A Practical Guide
to the MMPI

A Practical Guide to the MMPI

An Introduction for Psychologists, Physicians, Social Workers, and Other Professionals

by
Patricia King-Ellison Good
and
John P. Brantner

University of Minnesota Press
Minneapolis

Library of Congress Catalog Card Number: 61-18081

ISBN 8166-0706-0

An earlier edition of this work
appeared under the title *The
Physician's Guide to the MMPI.*

Acknowledgments

This volume was developed as an expansion of *The Physician's Guide to the MMPI,* published in 1961, following experience gained in using the *Physician's Guide* in teaching and clinical practice. We discovered, too, that the *Physician's Guide* was being extensively used by professionals other than physicians and this became an important consideration in the revision along with bringing the materials up to date as much as possible.

We are grateful for the comments of many colleagues and friends regarding their experiences with the *Physician's Guide* and for their help as we prepared this revision. Again, we have used material from many sources, especially the *Basic Readings on the MMPI in Psychology and Medicine,* edited by Welsh and Dahlstrom, *An MMPI Handbook,* revised edition, by Dahlstrom, Welsh, and Dahlstrom, *The Actuarial Description of Abnormal Personality* by Marks and Seeman, and a *Handbook for Clinical and Actuarial MMPI Interpretation* by Gilberstadt and Duker.

Patricia King-Ellison Good
John P. Brantner

Minneapolis, Minnesota
October 1973

Contents

A Practical Guide
to the MMPI

1

Introduction

The Minnesota Multiphasic Personality Inventory, familiarly known as the MMPI, appeared in the early 1940s as a new kind of psychometric tool for those concerned professionally with the assessment of personality. First used in psychiatric practice, the test in succeeding years proved adaptable to many other settings and today has a well-established place in such diverse fields as counseling, industry, medicine, and education. In addition, it is much used in research of various kinds.

This broad application has led to the accumulation of large amounts of reference data and to the development of many new and subtle concepts which have enriched interpretation of the MMPI immeasurably. The very magnitude and complexity of material available may, however, be discouraging to one who is just beginning to use the test. This *Guide* is intended to assist beginners as a text in conjunction with coursework or in self-study during the early learning period when it is necessary to concentrate on the simplest level of test use. It will serve also as a brief reference source for later clinical practice.

Independent use of the MMPI is restricted to qualified psychologists and to physicians. But many other professionals in the health care system and in the educational system have access to MMPI profiles on some of their clients. This book will serve as an introduction for those − whether psychologists, physicians, or other professionals − whose formal training did not include detailed information on the use of this specific psychological test, providing background for understanding its potential contribution and a guide for applications in specific instances.

3

If possible, of course, supervised learning in a professional setting is best for the practitioner with the MMPI, whatever his field. But for many the alternative of self-instruction is the only practical course. Physicians for example cannot usually learn to use the MMPI under supervised guidance. At most they will have the benefit of an introductory course on the test during their training in medical school or perhaps a brief seminar in an extension education center. Thereafter they must rely on their own cumulative independent experience, checked against and extended by whatever reading they are able to do. This can be a very successful learning method if the individual has the patience and determination to master the necessary rudimentary skills and then to build up a broad base of experience with test results from as many people as possible.

This *Guide*, then, brings together research results as well as some of the more widely held clinical opinions about test interpretation. For the physician and psychologist beginning their experience with the test it speaks to primary matters of availability, administration, and interpretation. For these and for those others who use test results in an institutional setting (schools, hospitals, counseling centers, etc.) the *Guide* will also teach clinical application of the test.

This *Guide* can, of course, only be an introduction to the MMPI. Fortunately, there is a whole shelf of volumes the test user can and should turn to as he explores the many facets of the test. The *MMPI Handbook* by Dahlstrom, Welsh, and Dahlstrom (two volumes in the revised edition, 1972 and 1974) is the most complete source of information about the MMPI. An annotated and descriptive list of other major references appears at the end of this *Guide*.

The MMPI consists of 550 statements covering a wide range of subject matter — from the physical condition of the person being tested to moral and social attitudes. The subject is asked to sort all the statements into one of three categories: True, False, and Cannot Say. The fundamental assumption underlying use of the test is that people behave consistently. That is, sad people will express their sorrow in their facial expressions, their posture, their appetite and sleeping behavior, their social behavior, their conversation — and in the way they answer MMPI items. In responding to the MMPI it does not matter whether or not they say things that are objectively true, or even things that have an obvious relationship to sadness. They will respond T and F in much the same way as do depressed patients. And the MMPI profile will reflect their depression and its seriousness. The scores, then, are one way of learning about individuals. Sometimes they can compensate for lack of time, skill, or experience on the part of the professional being consulted.

To make comparisons between people easier — since 550 variables of behavior are rather too many to be handled effectively one by one — the statements, or items as they are called, are grouped into scales for scoring purposes. After certain of the subject's responses have been counted for each scale, his scores are translated into a profile graph or into a "code."

There are a great many scales that may be scored — more than 450 have been used for one purpose or another. The basic ones are four validity scales and nine clinical scales. These are discussed in some detail in Chapters 3 and 4. A few of the optional scales are the subject of Chapter 5.

One general point should be made about the clinical scales. They were originally developed by selecting statements which distinguished certain psychiatric patients who had been classified into common, identifiable syndromes from a group of over a thousand persons selected as representative of the "normal" Minnesota population. These scales were originally named for the syndromes identified (except the fifth, for which the name adopted was a more general descriptive term): Hypochondriasis, Depression, Hysteria, Psychopathic Deviate, Masculinity-Femininity, Paranoia, Psychasthenia, Schizophrenia, and Hypomania. As the MMPI has been used more and more with groups from the general population, however, the psychiatric nomenclature has become inappropriate. While the scales do identify certain variables characteristic of most psychiatric patients diagnosed as hypochondriacal, depressed, and so on, they also identify aspects of personality falling in the "normal" range. For this reason, as well as for brevity, it is customary to refer to the clinical scales by an abbreviation or — better — by a number: Hs (1), D (2), Hy (3), Pd (4), Mf (5), Pa (6), Pt (7), Sc (8), Ma (9).

The use of numbers for the scales is especially desirable since it permits coding of scores, a kind of shorthand that makes it possible to classify large bodies of data for easy reference. Coding also helps to emphasize the importance of configural analysis in working with MMPI results; that is, instead of interpreting a subject's score on each scale separately, the relation of the scales to each other in his profile, their *pattern*, is the major consideration. For one just beginning work with the MMPI this relationship may perhaps be most easily seen in a profile graph, linking pictorially the several scale elevations for a subject. But graphs are time-consuming to prepare and difficult to consult in large numbers. Codes can be equally if not more illuminating and simplify problems in classification and reference. The procedure for coding is described in Chapter 2. Chapter 6 provides an introduction to configural interpretation.

Two further points should be noted before continuing into the more specific subject matter of the next chapters. The MMPI can by itself be a helpful source of hypotheses about and insights into the personality of an individual, but its most effective use is in combination with other information about that individual — if age, sex, education, occupation, and the like are known and clinical observations are available, as well as test results, any analysis and predictions will obviously be much more accurate than if one kind of information alone is relied on. It is also important to remember that the interpretative materials that follow are presented as tentative *hypotheses* to be modified in the light of the particular case rather than as absolute and unvarying facts applicable to every person. The application of these hypotheses depends on the overall configuration and validity of the profile, the relative and absolute values of the scores, and the nature of the particular population or the observable characteristics of the individual to whom the test has been administered.

2

Administration and Scoring

A number of forms of the MMPI are available: the box form and various booklet forms.* All forms can be used with literate subjects over age 15 (many 13 and over can take the test). In the box form the items are printed on individual cards which the subject sorts into the categories and which must generally be scored by hand. There are at least two booklet forms available at the present time, and a variety of answer sheets. The booklet forms require the use of a separate answer sheet and may be somewhat difficult for a person of limited experience or education to use. In group testing of high school or college students or educated adults the booklet forms will yield valid results for most subjects. A standard booklet is available which may be used with most of the special answer sheets and for hand scoring. Basically, the requirements of the chosen scoring system will dictate the choice of answer sheet forms. Form R, a new form, combines booklet and separate answer sheets in a stiff cover that serves as a writing surface.

Although there may be a few occasions when people will react negatively, the average person will accept the test as one of the procedures that will help a psychologist, physician, or other professional person to understand his case. It is very important that the test taker should not feel that the use of the MMPI will either bring about rejection or imply a judgment of mental illness. He or she will be spending considerable time in taking the test and should be able to expect some benefit from it. However, the person should not be led to expect an

---

*Qualified users may obtain copies from the Psychological Corporation, Test Division, 304 East 45th Street, New York, N.Y. 10017.

interpretation or a look at the scores (see Chapter 7). In some cases a modified interpretation may usefully be discussed with him.

Both the box form and the booklet forms are relatively easy to administer, but it is always undesirable simply to hand the test and written directions to the patient without comment. Most forms require some test-taking sophistication. The box form requires the least. For most subjects Form R will be most convenient. Instructions for administration and use of the answer sheets accompany most forms.

In some cases special effort may be necessary to secure cooperation. It may be helpful then to supplement the standard directions with the following comments. These should ordinarily be given by someone who can modify them to meet the person's understanding.

"The MMPI is a standard and well-known personality questionnaire intended to show important features of a person's psychology. The answers to the items are put into a machine which combines them into twelve or more scores or grades from selected *groupings* of items. These scores have been shown to be helpful to properly trained people as they seek to understand and advise others. To prepare a chart for use, the scores provided by the machine make a graph or 'profile.' That is all the trained person needs to read the meaning of the test. The answers to the separate questions are not read or used for this purpose. Every item should be answered as well as possible but no one or two items determine the meaning of your tests. Some items are hard to answer or don't seem to apply. Such items should be answered in any case even if the answer is a guess.

"It is best to say simply what seems most nearly true instead of worrying about what ought to be true. The profile of the test has grades that show if unreasonably good or bad things are said in making the answers. If answers are carelessly made or if they are not correct for the person making the test the profile is spoiled and the test may have to be repeated.

"Answers should not be compared to those of other persons nor should any other person be consulted in answering. The results from the test are confidential. The answer sheets and profiles are positively not available except to authorized people."

It is preferable to have a quiet unused room where the person can take the test without disturbance; this might be an empty examining room, a library, or a small room set aside for such uses. If such arrangements are not possible and the waiting room is not crowded the person might sit in a quiet corner. He should in any case be asked not to discuss the test with anyone while he is working on it.

The MMPI is well suited for routine use such as might be desirable in an educational or institutional setting or as part of the standard procedure for new patients or for complete periodic physical examinations. The booklet forms of the test can be used for administration in small groups, and any form of the test can be given to a patient in office practice.

Machine scoring is available for most booklet forms of the test. See the current catalogue of the Psychological Corporation, Test Division, for further details. Hand scoring can be done in those rare cases where immediate results are necessary. Reference to the appropriate manuals will instruct in the necessary procedures.

T Scores

For most purposes T scores are used in reporting MMPI results. These are one variety of derived, standard scores which permit the comparison of scores on various scales in relation to the same normative group. The following is the formula used to compute T scores:

$$T = 50 + \frac{10(X - M)}{S.D.}$$

where X is the raw score and M and S.D. the mean and standard deviation of the raw scores for the normative group. This adjusts the scores so that each scale has a mean of 50 and a standard deviation of 10.

Coding

Since the original coding system was proposed by Hathaway (see Welsh and Dahlstrom, 1956, Article 12) several other methods have been suggested including that of Welsh (see Welsh and Dahlstrom, 1956,

Article 13). Some of the later systems have the advantage of giving the data more precisely, but it is a modification of the Hathaway system (now in use at the University of Minnesota Hospitals) that will be described here since familiarity with it will permit easy use of the clinical *Atlas* (Hathaway and Meehl, 1951a — see the annotation in the reference list at the end of this *Guide*).

To code a profile the number-name must be used for each of the scales:

Hs = 1	Pd = 4	Pt = 7
D = 2	Mf = 5	Sc = 8
Hy = 3	Pa = 6	Ma = 9

(The Mf scale (5) is not, however, coded in this system; see step 8 below.) The following are the steps carried out:

1. Write down the number of that scale having the largest T score.

2. Write after this in descending order of T-score value the numbers of any other scales having T values greater than 54.

3. Insert a prime (′) at the point where the profile crosses the 70 T score. Thus, if the highest point is Pd (scale 4) and this is at 70 or greater T score, no other score being as large as 70, the prime would be written after a 4 and ahead of any numbers of scales that occur between 70 and 54 T scores.

4. If the T-score value on any scale is 80 or higher, this is set off by a double prime (″); similarly scores 90 or over would be set off by a triple prime (‴), 100 or over by four primes, etc.

5. Next underline all adjacent scale numbers where the T scores of the given scales are equal or within one point of each other. The underlining simply indicates that the scales are negligibly, or not at all, different in value. It is obvious that such scales have no absolute order in the code; but conventionally, if one is one point higher than the other, the number of that scale is placed first. If two or more scales are of absolutely equal T-score value, then the numbers of those scales are written in their usual ordinal sequence.

The symbols now written represent what is called the "high-point code" of the profile. The numbers show approximately the magnitude and order of all scales having T scores larger than 54.

6. After the high-point code, place a dash, and after the dash write the number of the lowest scale on the profile if that scale has a T score less than 46. Following the number of this scale, write in ascending order the numbers of any other scales whose T scores lie between this lowest one and 46. If any of the scores are below a T-score value of 40, these should be set off by a prime ('); similarly those below 30 should be set off by a double prime (").

7. Follow the same rule for underlining as is given in step 5. The code written to the right of the dash is called the "low-point code."

8. Following the low-point code, the T-score value of the Mf scale is given in parentheses, and this is followed by a superscript number, indicating how many items there are in the Cannot Say category. If for any of several reasons the profile is of doubtful validity, the Mf score should be preceded by an "X."

9. Finally, the raw scores on the L, F, and K scales are written in that order, separated by commas.

An example may be helpful. If Hs(1) = 39, D(2) = 43, Hy(3) = 52, Pd(4) = 86, Mf(5) = 45, Pa(6) = 61, Pt(7) = 53, Sc(8) = 60, Ma(9) = 71, raw ? = 0, raw L = 1, and raw F = 6, the code would be $4''9'\underline{68}-1'2(45)^0$ 1, 6, 13.

The alternative and frequently used coding system designed by Welsh is discussed in the *Handbook*, volume I (pages 72-74). For purposes of record keeping and research, there are advantages to both systems. The practices of specific institutions should be consulted. For interpretation of high-point codes the two systems are essentially similar in that the high points appear from left to right in order of relative elevation.

For ready reference in the chapters that follow the code designations of the validity and clinical scales and the letter designations of the special scales will be printed in boldface type.

3

The Validity Scales

The interpretation of the profile begins with the problem of validity. Did the subject understand what he read? Was he in a cooperative frame of mind or was he careless or reluctant to answer questions candidly? Did he try to "fake" a favorable or an unfavorable picture of himself by distorting his answers?

The **?**, **L**, **F**, and **K** scores act as a check on factors like literacy and attitude that may have influenced the scores of the subject on the various clinical scales and hence may have affected the validity of the whole profile. However, the problem of validity begins even earlier with the basic decisions of whether to use the test, how and by whom it is administered, and what kind of directions are given with it. In some settings the test is given routinely to everyone who is physically able to take it in some manner. In such cases it is important for the test giver to note how long the patient took to complete the test, whether he required any assistance in taking it, and whether he showed any unusual behavior while taking it. In other instances, it is probably more saving of time and money to give the test only to individuals who show sufficient intelligence, reading ability, and cooperativeness to produce a reasonably valid profile. This can usually be ascertained in a brief conversation with the subject about the nature, meaning, and purpose of the test. Many clinicians would prefer to keep the directions neutral in order to avoid influencing the results of the test (it is possible to influence the validity scores and the profile as well by giving directions which are too pointed in one direction or another) but then they run the risk of finding more invalid or "difficult to interpret" profiles. In

Chapter 2 an example of test directions which are relatively neutral or objective is given.

? (Cannot Say) Scale

The ? scale is based on the number of items placed by the subject in the Cannot Say category (box form) or left unanswered (booklet form). Although T scores have been given for this scale, in ordinary clinical practice it is desirable that no more than 10 items be left unanswered. Most subjects are compliant if asked to limit their unanswered items to fewer than 10, and in some settings the choice of Cannot Say is omitted entirely, either by leaving out the ? card in the box form or by instructing subjects to answer all items in the booklet form, with no difficulty at all. In any case, the person administering the test can mention that it will be understood that any item may not be completely or altogether true or false as the case may be, but that the subject is merely indicating the predominance of his feelings about the item.

In situations where the person interpreting or using the test did not administer the test, it is desirable to have some information about how the test was administered and how the individual responded. If this information is not available the clinician is in the difficult position of trying to decide whether a profile is usable. The new R form of the test, although very convenient for use in many settings including the doctor's office, does present some additional problems in connection with the Cannot Say category. It is generally harder for a person to omit an item and come back to it later because the spaces are not numbered on the answer sheet and it is sometimes difficult to line up the correct answer space with a given item. One can be insistent that the test taker answer all the items on each page before turning to the next page without spending much time on them, although then one risks the chance that the person will be less careful in answering the items than he should be or may stick to a particular kind of "response set" which might affect the other validity scores.

Occasionally, a somewhat defensive or depressed person or one who uses intellectual defenses excessively may be unable to decide whether a great number of items are true or false, giving lengthy or involved reasons for his inability to make up his mind. In this case the direction to answer the items as they are mostly true or mostly false can be repeated. If the person is still unable to decide, this fact alone has considerable diagnostic significance.

Some clinicians, when a large number of items have been left unanswered, arbitrarily score these items on each of the clinical scales as if they had been answered in the significant direction. Although this procedure may help in indicating the maximum strength of various symptom patterns, *it renders the standardization table invalid and might change the interpretation.* In most cases it will result in practically no change in the shape and only slightly in the elevation of the profile. It is most useful in the few cases where the unanswered items are concerned primarily with a single subject area such as sex, family problems, or religion, or where the unanswered items are heavily concentrated on one or two scales.

Special Considerations in Interpreting L, F, and K

The chief difficulty in interpreting **L, F,** and **K** scores lies in the fact that they have two levels of meaning. Most obviously they provide a measure of the validity of the scores on the clinical scales by indicating the general test-taking competency of the subject and his test-taking attitude. But that attitude is itself an aspect of the subject's personality as well as an influence on validity. If he is defensive or overcandid, or if he rejects items related to symptoms of his difficulty, the validity indicator that betrays him tells us something about the kind of person he is. Interpretation of these scales must then be concerned with both the effect of the subject's attitude on the value of the clinical scales and implications of that attitude for the assessment of his personality. If one uses instructions designed to increase the likelihood of valid test results, one runs the risk of losing some of this secondary kind of information.

Another factor to consider in the question of validity is the setting or circumstances for the test. Although the subject's interpretation of the setting may vary considerably, there are certain circumstances which might favor certain kinds of responses. For example, in an assessment or selection situation the individual might be impressed with the need to look as normal (or as sick) as possible. In certain outpatient settings the patient may give test results suggesting extreme problems because he is trying to get help at that point. On the other hand, the same person when hospitalized may feel more comfortable and secure and look much less disturbed on his test profile. Although one may not always know the circumstances of the testing or the subject's interpretation of it, it is important to have as many of the obvious facts as possible before interpreting the profile. Similarly, if a profile is sent to another clinician or to a computer service for interpretation, any pertinent information of this type should be included instead of expecting that the clinician can make inferences simply from the profile.

L Scale

The **L** scale consists of 15 items concerned with minor but nearly universal faults. Some examples of the general type of **L** items are these: "I sometimes tell white lies," "Once in a while I am lazy," and "Sometimes I do things I shouldn't do." Although the usual correct answer is True, it is more socially acceptable to say False. Presumably, subjects who want to place themselves in a desirable light will obtain a high **L** score by distorting their responses to these items. Experience with the test points to **L** scores of 60 and higher as probable indications of this tendency. **L** scores of 70 and larger are almost certain indicators of this type of invalid response.

A high **L** score usually indicates a relative invalidity of the profile: the subject has suppressed or misrepresented certain material in the "fake good" direction so that certain scale elevations are lower than they would be if he had been frank. However, in some cases, despite the high **L**, a subject will still obtain high scores on one or more of the clinical scales. These are probably a proper and valid measurement, even though one must recognize that the overall configuration has been distorted to some degree. Further questioning of the subject will usually reveal more about the material he is attempting to conceal.

High scores on **L** are likely to reflect only the more crude and brazen attempts at test distortion. This kind of test distortion is usually resorted to only by persons with limited sophistication or proficiency in dealing with psychological tests and who have below average intellectual or educational levels, or histories of socioeconomic or cultural deprivation.

Valid elevations of the **L** score in the high to markedly elevated range may be generated by persons who are honestly describing themselves as they see themselves. They tend to be overly conventional, socially conforming, and prosaic. Some of the descriptions actually correspond to their habitual patterns of behavior while other features of their test answers reflect their poor insight and limited self-knowledge. That is, they may be highly religious and moralistic individuals who rigidly control any overt expression of antisocial or unethical impulses. At the same time, they may be expressing some of these tendencies without being aware of the impact that their behavior may have upon others or without recognizing their own motives and purposes. Thus, elevated **L**-scale values are likely in some test subjects who are ministers, reformers, social activists, or evangelical missionaries. Persons with borderline paranoid reactions may answer many **L** items in the defensive direction because of their grandiose view of themselves and the perfectionism that they must ascribe to themselves. Other conditions which generate serious limitations in self-insight are also related to elevations on the **L** scale, particularly hysteroid defensive mechanisms and elaborate hypochondriacal reactions.

Low-range scores have not been studied extensively, but available evidence indicates that all or most of the **L**-scale items may be answered True by persons attempting to create an extremely pathological picture of themselves on the test. Scores in the low range are also earned by normal persons who are relatively unconventional, independent, and self-reliant and are merely unusually free in acknowledging such social foibles. Brighter, more highly educated, and more knowledgeable subjects may avoid **L**-scale items in their efforts to create both a favorable and a believable image on this test. These normal subjects may answer items of the **K** scale in a defensive way while freely acknowledging the negative attributes in the **L**-scale items.

F Scale

The **F** scale is made up of items observed to be rarely answered in the scaled direction by normal persons. The items were also chosen to include a variety of content so that it would be unlikely any one individual would answer many of the items in the unusual direction. Out of 64 items, the ordinary person will usually receive a raw score of 7 or less (50 percent of normal subjects have a score of 3 or less). Whenever a subject does not answer with discrimination because of inability to read and understand well enough, direct carelessness, or carelessness with intent to confuse the data, the score on the **F** scale will be elevated. The higher the **F** score, the more likely it is that some factor has operated to invalidate the whole test. The simplest interpretations of a high score are that the subject failed to understand the items, that he didn't cooperate properly, or that extensive clerical errors occurred in scoring the scales. A T score of 70 or less on **F** is a comfortable assurance that the subject has cooperated and understood to a reasonable degree and that scoring has been reasonably accurate. Beyond the simple interpretation of the **F** scale, however, it must be kept in mind that this score also rises with psychological illnesses of certain types; schizoid and depressed patients are particularly likely to obtain a high **F** score even if they answered carefully and with an acceptable attitude.

It is probably safe to say that T scores from 70 to 80 do not usually represent invalidity of the simpler types indicated above, but such high scores are always adequate cause for question. Any interpretation of a profile that has a high **F** must be dependent upon direct assurance that the **F** was not due to carelessness of the subject or to scoring errors. At times it may be feasible to interview the subject and even to ask him directly if he had been careful in answering and if he understood what he was doing. Sometimes a few items can be gone over to test his comprehension. More often, the evaluation of high **F** profiles will have to depend upon the overall appearance of the rest of the profile. Generally speaking, when an elevated **F** indicates carelessness or failure to cooperate on the part of the subject, most of the other scales will also be elevated above 70; scale **1** is particularly unlikely to be as low as 55 in such cases. To a certain extent all the scales, with the exception of **5**, act as **F** does when the MMPI is invalidly responded to; that is, all scales tend to go up.

It is useful to collect examples obtained by random sorting with various proportions of items answered True and False. Generally, when the raw **F** is between 26 and 38, the possibility of a randomly sorted test is very high. If the raw **F** score is much higher than 40, the possibility that the True and False responses were in some way reversed should be investigated.

Scale **F** also indicates when a subject has chosen, consciously or unconsciously, to put himself in a very bad light. Subjects who wish to feign serious mental disturbance or who wish to be considered ill in some degree may distort scales to an extreme degree. In doing this, they are apt to obtain high **F** scores, and the majority of them will invalidate the profile on that basis. Among persons who are in considerable psychological distress a high **F** score may be interpreted as a "plea for help" or an attempt to call attention to their psychological difficulties. Very compulsive persons who are trying hard to be frank may obtain moderate or high scores on **F** by being overly self-critical.

Moderately high scores on **F** may be obtained by persons in special circumstances such as being involved in radical or extremist political movements, participating in deviant religious sects, or having unusual or severe health problems. If a person is going through a phase of rebellion against his family or their values he may obtain an elevation on **F**. Some of the **F**-scale items also bear upon delinquent acts or experiences encountered when one is treated as a juvenile delinquent in current police or court procedures.

Among persons relatively free of psychopathology, those with moderate elevations on **F** have been described as moody, restive, curious, changeable, dissatisfied, restless, talkative, complex, unstable, opinionated, affected, and opportunistic. The inconsistency of these adjectives may reflect some of the considerations above as well as the fact that one may obtain a high **F** score for many reasons.

Low scores on **F** may reflect a systematic tendency to avoid endorsement of socially unacceptable, threatening, or disturbing content among the test items. Efforts to hide serious psychopathology and deliberately fake a good test record may lead to very low **F**-scale scores.

This can usually be checked out by the other validity scores and the pattern generated by the clinical scales. Normals with low **F** scores have been described as unassuming and unpretentious, simple and sincere, moderate, honest, slow, calm, and dependable. Their life-style usually involves few protestations, little social friction, and general compatibility with and accommodation to their present situation.

K Scale

Generally, the **K** score is thought of as a measure of test-taking attitude related to the **L** and **F** attitudes, but somewhat subtler and probably tapping a slightly different set of distorting factors. High **K** scores (over 60) represent defensiveness against psychological weaknesses, and, like the high **L** score, may indicate a defensiveness that verges upon deliberate distortion in the good direction. A low **K** score (under 45) indicates the person's defenses are down, that he is, if anything, overly candid and self-critical and likely to express symptoms even though these may be minimal in strength. A low **K** score, like the high **F**, can also result from a deliberate intent to obtain bad scores or to make a bad impression.

Various research studies suggest that **K** scores are positively related to personality characteristics such as self-management, personal effectiveness, healthy personal insight and self-understanding, and personality integration and control. **K** is also positively related to socioeconomic status and educational level, so that fairly high **K** scores may be obtained in college-level subjects who are well adjusted, self-reliant, and easily capable of dealing with their day-to-day problems. High **K** persons have been described as sociable, good mixers, reasonable, enthusiastic, verbal, enterprising, ingenious, resourceful, versatile, and having wide interests.

The **K** correction is used with clinical scales **1**, **4**, **7**, **8**, and **9**. Since the **K** corrections are statistics derived from the general population, they may not apply equally well to all groups, particularly to such groups as college students for whom the average **K** score tends to be above that of the general population. However, the clinician cannot attempt to change the **K** correction for each subgroup of the population that is dealt with; it is easier to use the standard **K** correction and

n mind the characteristics of the particular group with which he is
king. In cases where the T score on the **K** scale is higher than 70,
he should be cautious in making a detailed evaluation of the clinical
scales without further information about the subject. With scales **1**, **7**,
and **8** it is important also to look at the raw scores before making an
interpretation. There is some indication that the **K** correction for scale
4 is inappropriate for black populations. The **K** correction may increase
the intercorrelation between scales such as **1** and **3**, and **7** and **8**, so that
certain diagnostic distinctions are occasionally more difficult.

There is considerable clinical interest in the **K** variable as a measure
in its own right. The experience of some clinicians has indicated that
patients who are open to therapeutic work and are ready to accept help
have average or low **K**'s; conversely, persons strongly resistant to change
or to developing clinically useful dependence are likely to have **K** scores
of 65 or above. There is also some indication that as a patient "gets
hold of himself" and apparently gets better, although often without a
basic change in his pattern of difficulty, he will show a higher **K** on
retest. It is, of course, important to determine if, after a stay in the
hospital or extended psychotherapy, the person has some motivation
for wishing to appear better even though his basic problems have not
been resolved.

Low **K** scores when not the result of deliberate faking may suggest a
person of limited educational experience, deprived family background,
small-town or rural origins, low occupational status, or limited income.
They may have many problems – financial, interpersonal, occupational
– which they are willing to admit and delineate at length on the test.
Studies of normals with low **K** scores indicate that they may have a
poor self-concept, be strongly self-dissatisfied, but be lacking either the
self-managing techniques or the interpersonal skills that would enable
them to improve their lot in the world. They have been described as
conforming, cautious, awkward, inhibited, peaceable, retiring, shallow,
dissatisfied, high-strung, cynical, and individualistic.

K+ Profile (K-Plus)

Marks and Seeman have described the **K+** profile as applying only to
psychiatric inpatients who have all clinical scales below 70 and at least

six of the clinical scales below 60 T score. These profiles have both **L** and **K** greater than **F**, with **F** below 60 and **K** − **F** (raw scores) more than 5 T-score points. These people are described as shy, anxious, and inhibited. They are defensive about admitting psychological conflicts and afraid of emotional involvement with others; they keep people at a distance and avoid close interpersonal relationships. They tend not to become involved in things, are passively resistant, but are also suggestible and overly responsive to other people's evaluations rather than their own. About half of these people were diagnosed as mixed schizophrenic, with chronic brain disorders in 24 percent, obsessive-compulsive in 14 percent, and sociopathic in 14 percent of the population. These people had above average school achievement and educational attainment even though a significant proportion came from homes marked by poverty, disruption, or death of a parent. They generally had good marital adjustments, and very rarely showed any delinquent or criminal behavior. They were described also as suspicious, paranoid, hostile, withdrawn, and phobic with somatic complaints, sleep disturbances, and sexual difficulties. Most of them made some improvement with psychotherapy only and had fair to poor prognoses.

F − K Index

Gough (see Welsh and Dahlstrom, 1956, Article 35) has suggested that the raw score on **F** minus the raw score on **K** should be used as a main indicator of test-taking distortions. He found that a difference (**F** − **K**) of 9 or more would identify a large proportion of profiles distorted in the unfavorable direction − that is, the so-called false-positive or "plus-getting" profiles in which normal subjects try to respond to the test items like, say, hospitalized psychotics. However, the efficacy of any particular cutting score is likely to vary depending upon the particular population involved. And while experience has shown the validity scores to be quite effective in detecting false-positive profiles, they have proved definitely less effective detectors when distortion occurs in the good or "normal" direction.

In this connection, experienced users of the MMPI have tended to modify their thinking about the validity scores by attention to the clinical profile itself. High **F** scores, for example, are unlikely to be an tion of scoring error or of deliberate adverse falsification of a profile if there are T scores near 50 for several of the clinical scales. In the other direction, profiles with many low scores may be regarded with some suspicion even though the **L** and **K** scores are not greatly elevated.

If **F** – **K** is highly negative (**F** – **K** < -11, i.e., -12, -13, -14, etc.) in the nonpsychiatric patient, this may reflect a general inability to share distress with others. These people do not make physical complaints, they assume an outwardly serene appearance even when very uncomfortable, and they are generally uncomplaining and cooperative. When this response is combined with depression and inactivity, recovery from physical illness is slower and response to treatment is poorer.

4

The Clinical Scales

As mentioned in Chapter 1 the nine clinical scales were originally developed by choosing those items which discriminated a group of psychiatric patients with a given diagnosis or syndrome from a normal group. In some cases such as scale 8, it was necessary to try out several scales or combinations of scales to find one with the maximum discriminating power. Since several other sources including the *Manual* (Hathaway and McKinley, 1967) and the *Handbook* (volume I, Dahlstrom, Welsh, and Dahlstrom, 1972) discuss the actual diagnostic groups, this chapter will not repeat that material, but rather will discuss the clinical uses of the scales. As mentioned previously too, the clinical scales have been found to have many connotations besides the original one of psychiatric syndrome. In fact, if the scales are used without regard to these other meanings, serious errors may be made.

Some of the material in the chapter is taken from studies which noted characteristics typical of high and low scorers on the various scales. Other studies described persons for whom the particular scale was the highest score or "peak" on the profile. These sources are also discussed at greater length in the *Handbook*. The original sources include Drake and Oetting (1959), Hathaway and Monachesi (1953, 1963), Hathaway and Meehl (1951b, 1952), Guthrie (1949), Mello and Guthrie (1958), Drake (1956), Black (1953), Gilberstadt and Duker (1965), and Wiener and Harmon (1946).

Although not much is known about the low scores (45 or below) on the clinical scales, except for scale 5, a few brief comments and tentative interpretations are included here. The table in the clinical *Atlas*

(Hathaway and Meehl, 1951a) giving the frequencies of various high-point and low-point combinations for different populations may be of interest in this area. Drake and Oetting provide some material on the effect of various low points on the profiles of college student counselees. Since it is highly desirable for users of the MMPI to think of the scales in terms of their code numbers instead of their psychiatric syndrome names, we shall use the numbers in the discussion that follows so that they will become familiar and be associated with the descriptive material. A tenth scale, Si (coded **0**) is often included among the basic clinical scales, but we shall defer discussion of it to Chapter 5.

Scale 1 (Hs)

It appears to be most useful to think of scale **1** as a measure of somatic concern or as an index of the importance of bodily functions and symptoms to the particular person. Persons with high scores tend to deny good health, both by endorsing explicit symptoms and by acknowledging a large variety of rather vague somatic complaints. There may be many complaints about pains or disorders which are difficult to identify and for which no clear organic basis can be found. The items on scale **1** range over a variety of bodily complaints; they include generalized aches and pains, specific complaints about digestion, breathing, thinking, vision, and sleep as well as peculiarities of sensation. A few of the items relate to general health or competence. Since the items on scale **1** are so obvious, a correction factor of .5 K is used as an index of unwillingness to verbalize such obvious symptomatology. In some populations this correction factor may be inappropriate so one should also check the raw score on scale **1**; generally a raw score over 10 would be indicative of undue somatic concern.

Although patients with definite medical problems will also obtain elevations on scale **1**, elevations over T score of 65 or raw score of 10 would suggest a psychological component or exaggerated somatic concern even in patients who are physically very ill. This elevation on scale **1** is an indication of the patient's need for at least some therapeutic reassurance about his physical condition and perhaps for more direct psychotherapeutic attention to his emotional difficulties.

In studies of personality correlates of scale **1**, the results vary a good deal, depending on the particular population studied and concomitant elevations of other scales, indicating that there may not be any pure set of personality variables correlated with scale **1** except for the degree of somatic concern mentioned above. As will be seen later, however, in the discussion of various two- and three-digit codes, the relative relationship between **1** and other scale elevations can be of crucial diagnostic importance.

Guthrie found that medical patients with the highest score or peak on scale **1** typically reported a wide variety of symptoms and complaints. Usually these patients did not show much manifest anxiety, but when anxiety was present it tended to predict favorable response to treatment. Most of these people did not show marked incapacity but rather functioned with somewhat reduced efficiency. Their symptoms appeared related to long-standing inadequacy and ineffectualness rather than to an immediate pressing problem.

Elevations of scale **1** are probably sufficiently uncommon among adolescents and young adults to merit some attention regardless of the rest of the profile. Among college women counselees, scale **1** was associated with the complaint of headaches when combined with a low coding of scale **5**. Among adolescent boys, a high **1** score was associated with poor school conduct.

Among college counselees a low score on **1** appeared to intensify certain problems suggested by the high codings on other scales in the profile. For example, low **1** with high **5** or high **7** suggests home conflict. Otherwise, low **1** scores appear to be relatively rare outside of normal groups, so that a low **1** score may have a limited clinical usefulness. In normals it does seem to be indicative of a general sense of well-being and good health and freedom from hampering neurotic inhibitions.

A high scale **1** represents neurotic concern in the areas of physical health and somatic complaints. A low scale **1** shows that the person does not employ this frequently useful and focusing mechanism. Consequently with low scale **1**, neurotic symptoms may be spread over a broader area and appear more numerous; problems represented by other elevations (i.e., **2**, **5**, **7**, etc.) may be intensified. A very low **1** (raw score 0 or 1 item) may be a reaction against hypochondriasis, or a self-image of perfect physical health, and is commonly observed in medical students, nursing students, and some athletes. In normals a scale 1 with raw scores of 3 to 6 indicates a general sense of well-being and good health and freedom from hampering somatic concerns.

Scale 2 (D)

Scale 2 appears to be a fairly sensitive index of mood and temporary changes in morale. Elevations on scale 2 suggest poor morale, feelings of uselessness, depression, dejection, discouragement, subjective distress, self-dissatisfaction, self-criticism, pessimism, hopelessness, and a tendency to worry.

The item content of scale 2 is quite varied. There are some items that deal with a lack of interest in things, expressed in a general apathy, in a rejection of base impulses, and in a distinct denial of happiness or personal worth. Other items describe a feeling of being incapable of performing work satisfactorily or of controlling one's thought processes. Another cluster of items indicating physical symptoms, sleep disturbance, and gastrointestinal complaints is not generally considered part of the depression syndrome but these features can very frequently be observed in markedly depressed psychiatric patients. The excessive sensitivity and lack of sociability reflected in these items can also be seen in the behavior of such patients.

Scale 2 does not differentiate the various kinds of depression or between chronic or temporary depression. The total configuration may be helpful, but often the person's history is a better guide to a differential diagnosis. However, the elevations on scale 2 seem to be closely related to the severity of the depression: T scores 60 to 70, mild; 70 to 80, moderate; 80 and over, severe. If the profile is valid a moderate to severe elevation of scale 2 should always call for professional attention in its own right; in the so-called "smiling depression" the person may deny depressive content and not show outward signs of depression but may still obtain a marked elevation on scale 2.

To some extent moderate but not extreme elevations on scale 2 may predict good response to treatment whether psychotherapy, ECT, treatment for organic disease, or even educational programs or environmental changes in less severe problems.

Adjective studies comparing high and low scores on scale **2** do not seem to give consistent results, possibly because the raters were not able to get to know the subjects very well. Hathaway and Meehl's study found the normal males were described as modest, sensitive, and individualistic and as having aesthetic interests. They also seemed to be dissatisfied generally, but particularly self-dissatisfied, as well as emotional, high-strung, and prone to worry. The women were described as high-strung, modest, frank, and intuitive.

Mello and Guthrie found that college counselees frequently had a peak on scale **2**. This seemed to reflect disturbance over situational problems in the college setting, such as relations with the opposite sex, studying, or vocational choice. While in therapy, these people resisted efforts of the therapists to go deeply into the origins of their problems; they used intellectualized statements or often-repeated descriptions of their problems to keep the therapy superficial. When the situational pressures let up, these counselees discontinued treatment quickly. Drake found that college counselees with peaks on **2** were characterized as unhappy or depressed particularly when scales **0**, **7**, or **8** were also elevated.

Hathaway and Monachesi found that a high point on scale **2** was rare in adolescent subjects and there were so few cases that they were not statistically different from the population in general.

Among medical patients with high points on scale **2** there was a high incidence of depression with some physical symptoms, but these were not prominent or varied. These patients tended to show a poor response to treatment. Some of the code combinations with scale **2** and other scales are discussed further in Chapter 6. Guthrie found that when scale **2** was the only codable scale and the low point was on scale **9**, the depression was mild and the physical complaints were rather typically centered around fatigue and loss of energy. These moderate physical complaints yielded rather easily to reassurance and symptomatic treatment. Occasionally a period of mild overactivity was reported to have occurred before the depressive symptoms appeared.

Low **2** scores may be fairly common in the "normal" population and are probably related to a sense of psychological well-being. There is probably a lack of depressive affect and a tendency to be cheerful and enthusiastic, but further interpretation depends on the rest of the profile and the person's situation. In certain situations such as those where the person has marital problems or problems with children or is chronically ill or disabled, a low **2** score may signify a rather poor prognosis for response to treatment.

Scale 3 (Hy)   hysteria

Scale **3** has two distinct components. The first consists of somatic complaints and is closely correlated with scale **1**. The second component, sometimes referred to as "Hy-subtle," seems to express an overcompensatory rejection of the possibility that the subject is capable of being neurotic and an attempt to show that he is unusually well socially. He claims that he does not tire easily and does not get depressed, that life about him is good, that he is having a good time and should be grateful for what the world offers him. He protests that other people are trustworthy, responsible, and likable. This component is probably seen in "normals" with high **3** scores, who are often optimistic and cheerful in the face of difficulties, using denial and rationalization. They tend to be well liked in superficial social relations, i.e., "their friends and acquaintances like them." To some extent the "Hy-subtle" component is also a measure of morale or a sense of well-being. Adolescent and college-age persons tend to have higher scores than the adult normative population.

Although this scale was originally developed to aid in the identification of patients using the neurotic defenses of the conversion form of hysteria, actual diagnostic distinctions must be made on the basis of combinations of **3** with other clinical scales. Much of this sort of information is found among the two- or three-digit codes discussed in Chapter 6.

Among Guthrie's group of medical patients, scale **3** was the most frequent high point and was commonly associated with a clinical picture of anxiety attacks. They suffered from occurrences of tachycardia, palpitation, and headaches. Home and marital maladjustments were common. They responded well to treatment including advice and reassurance, but some of the patients resented the suggestion of personality difficulties and failed to come back for scheduled visits. A fairly large subgroup had profiles where **3** was the only scale in the codable range. Their symptoms tended to be mild, generally involving the circulatory system, the upper gastrointestinal tract, or headaches. They sometimes complained of feeling nervous and tense but did not complain of other neurotic problems. They were more often seen for a general physical checkup than because they were ill or in distress.

Mello and Guthrie described high **3** college counselees as presenting problems rooted in an unhappy home situation, frequently involving a rejecting father to which a woman reacts with somatic complaints and a man with rebellion. Drake and Oetting found that the male college counselees with high **3**'s and low **0** scores showed good general adjustment particularly in social relations but also in verbal skills and in the ability to reason effectively. They also showed a tendency to aggressiveness and insistence upon direct answers in counseling. However, when scale **5** was also high they did not show this aggressiveness and were more dependent in the counseling situation. Among females, the high **3**, low **0** pattern indicated a socially outgoing and marriage-oriented girl, but when **5** was also low some physical complaints, such as headache and exhaustion, were noted. A high **7** along with high **3** and low **0** indicated a tendency for the girl to lack academic drive, to be anxious, and to have insomnia.

High **3** adolescents tend to show high intelligence, high achievement, and acceptance of middle-class values, according to Hathaway and Monachesi.

Low **3** scores tend to be associated with persons described as constricted, conventional, controlled, and having narrow interests. Low **3** scores did not appear to be significant among college counselees, but in high school they tended to indicate somewhat the opposite of high **3** scores, that is, low grades, low ability, and lower socioeconomic background.

Scale 4 (Pd)

Items on scale **4** can be grouped into a number of categories. Social maladjustment items are frequent, including statements referring to use of alcohol, sexual problems, previous episodes of petty thievery or difficulty with the law, and others suggesting difficulties in social situations. Related to these groups are the items referring to family difficulties. There are also items suggesting depression, the absence of strongly pleasant experience, and paranoid trends. Subtle and obvious subscales have been formed for scale **4**, and scale **4** items have been grouped into four clusters relating to family discord, authority problems, social imperturbability, social alienation, and self-alienation. Persons with high **4** scores are typically described as sociable, frank, talkative, adventurous, liking to drink, and individualistic. They may also show irresponsibility, undependability, tactlessness, egocentricity, hostility, and aggressiveness. Among normals the **4** elevation may represent a philosophical attitude, a willingness to challenge authority and the status quo, and independence of thought.

Elevations of scale **4** are extremely common among adolescents, and scores in the 70s should probably be considered in the normal range. This is probably consistent with their characteristic rebelliousness, questioning of moral standards, and attempt to achieve both financial and social independence from the family and other authority figures. The likelihood of adolescent delinquent behavior is highest when the **4** scale is elevated in combination with **6**, **8**, or **9** whereas scales **1**, **2**, **5**, or **7** tend to act as "repressor variables" so that delinquency is less likely when they are high.

Scale **4** elevations are common among many groups including alcoholics, homeless men, delinquent and prison groups, drivers with large numbers of traffic accidents and offenses, and drug abusers. In couples coming for marriage counseling scale **4** is the first or second high point in about 60 percent of the cases. Some of the common two-point codes including **4** are discussed in Chapter 6.

Scale **4** elevations among persons over 40 years old (except for alcoholics) are unlikely to indicate antisocial tendencies or impulsive acting out, especially in people in their seventies and eighties, but scale

4 elevations in the middle-aged and elderly are quite common. These scores seem to reflect social alienation, absence of pleasure, apathy, and lack of involvement and commitment, and are often associated with the post-family and post-vocation years.

When scale 4 is elevated in a profile dominated by another pattern such as 13 or 27, it may suggest feelings of hostility, aggression, family or marital problems, or feelings of social inadequacy. Scale 4 may indicate lack of control, and thus suggest an increased likelihood of the person acting out whatever pattern is present.

Medical patients with peak 4 scores were described by Guthrie as having some sort of social maladjustment in their histories, particularly when their second high score fell on scale 2, 3, 6, or 9. Men with this profile tended to be alcoholic, to gamble excessively, or to show poor work records. Among the women there were histories of recurrent marital difficulties and illegitimate pregnancies. Their symptoms were episodic in nature, mild in degree, and overshadowed by their behavioral difficulties. Since they were unreliable patients, their response to treatment was difficult to assess. Deep personality conflicts appeared in the groups with scale 7 or 8 in second place in the profile.

Low 4 scores, below 45, are rare among medical and psychiatric groups. In normal groups they tend to occur among conventional, conforming persons with a narrow range of interests and often religious, particularly fundamental Protestant, beliefs, who attend church regularly. Low 4 scores have also been associated with lack of heterosexual interest. Although this characteristic may appear in a variety of ways, the lack of effective expression of normal sexual interest seems pervasive.

Scale 5 (Mf)

Masculinity and femininity may be becoming somewhat outmoded concepts. They pertain more appropriately to the culture of the 1930s and possibly the 1950s, but scale 5 is a relatively good measure of these concepts. The item content of scale 5 is diverse, ranging over interests in kinds of work, hobbies and pastimes, social activities, religious preferences, family relationships, fears, worries, personal sensitivities, and frankly sexual material. One has to check out clinically whether a particular score is reflecting interest patterns, passivity-dependency dimensions, or some sexual concerns. Since scale **5** is scored in opposite directions for men and women the meanings of high and low scores are typically opposite also. The score on **5** is also affected by education and occupation and socioeconomic level.

High-scoring men tend to have greater interest in people, language, and ideas, as opposed to mechanical, computational, and scientific areas; they are also more inclined toward cultural and aesthetic (music, art, etc.) interests. They are described by others as sensitive and idealistic, and they tend to show greater sensitivity to their environment than low-scoring men and warmer feelings toward others. They may be somewhat inclined to be passive and dependent in their relationships with others and somewhat better able to recognize and express emotional feeling than other men. High scores on **5** have also been found related to the following descriptions of male subjects: clever, imaginative, insightful, intelligent, having wide interests, logical, mature, sensitive, introspective, concerned with himself as an object, self-aware, concerned with philosophical problems (i.e., religion, values, the meaning of life), taking stands on moral grounds, communicating ideas clearly.

Low **5** men tend to be interested in mechanical, computational, and scientific activities, as well as in sports and outdoor activities. They are described as easygoing, adventurous, relaxed, and having physical strength and endurance.

High **5** women tend to be somewhat like the low **5** men in interests and personality traits. They have also been characterized as driving, vigorous, and determined. Beyond the adolescent years high **5** scores are probably fairly uncommon in women. Among both men and women, a high **5** score may confirm a hypothesis of either dissatisfaction with or departure from traditional sex role patterns, or rarely homoerotic or homosexual tendencies.

Low **5** women tend to be like high **5** men in interests and personality traits. In psychiatric settings a very low score can suggest an almost masochistic passivity, and the combination of high **4** and low **5** (**6** sometimes high also — see the discussion of the **46** code type in Chapter

6) seems to characterize the passive-aggressive personality (males with **4, 5, 6** all coded high may be similar).

The **5** score probably has some usefulness in marriage counseling, but it is only significant of a "bad" marriage when the husband's score is 74 or more and the wife's score is 18 points lower, or as noted above when a **46** code is combined with a low **5** in the female or high **5** in the male.

Scale 6 (Pa)

Scale **6** can be considered an index of paranoid thinking including ideas of reference and persecution, grandiose self-concepts, suspiciousness, oversensitivity, and egotism. In the "normal" range it might suggest anger, resentment, hostility, or undue interpersonal sensitivity. The scale includes items with frankly psychotic content such as mental peculiarities, delusional and referential ideas, and the belief that unwarranted pressure has been placed upon the subjects. However, Wiener and Harmon have also identified a subtle portion of the **6** scale which involves an admission of psychological fragility as well as some items which seem to be a denial of suspiciousness or paranoid thinking.

"Normal" males with higher scores on **6** have been described as sensitive, emotional, prone to worry, kind, affectionate, generous, and grateful. The women have been described as emotional, softhearted, sensitive, frank, and high-strung. It is relatively rare that **6** is the highest scale on a profile but this is somewhat more frequent among adolescent females. College girls with **6** as the high point have been described as shrewd, hardhearted, clever, affected, poised, high-strung, and submissive. Among female college counselees a high point on **6** is sometimes associated with personal sensitivity about some physical defect. Adolescent girls with high **6** tend to have high intelligence and to get good grades; they are considered well adjusted by others and are often very popular. Guthrie's medical patients with peak scores on scale **6** typically presented complaints centered around the gastrointestinal tract. They established poor rapport with the physician, disliked talking about their emotional problems, and frequently did not return for follow-up visits. They had long-standing problems centering around hostility and resentment toward members of their families.

This scale is one of the weakest of the clinical scales in that paranoid persons are sometimes successful in avoiding betrayal of themselves on this scale and may even produce an almost flat profile with only a little elevation to give any clue at all. Many clinicians are especially alert for paranoid symptoms in psychiatric patients with normal MMPI profiles. However, persons who do obtain elevations over 70 on this scale are described as sensitive in relations with others and having poor interpersonal relationships, which often results in anger and resentment. This scale is most useful in combinations with other scales such as **86, 46, 36,** and **96.**

Some clinicians feel that low scores on **6** have implications similar to those for a high **6** score. Adjective studies of low scorers on scale **6** have had rather contradictory results although these people seem to have few social interests and skills. Among high school and college students low **6** scores are associated both with underachievement and with low ability and low achievement.

Scale 7 (Pt)

Scale **7** measures the similarity of the subject to psychiatric patients who are troubled by phobias or compulsions. The compulsive behavior may be either explicit, as expressed by excessive hand washing, vacillation, or other ineffectual activity, or implicit, as in the inability to escape useless thinking or obsessive ideas. The phobias include unreasonable fears of things or situations as well as overreaction to more reasonable stimuli. Also noted are excessively high standards of morality or intellectual performance, self-critical or even self-debasing feelings and attitudes, and assumption of rather remote and unemotional aloofness from some personal conflicts.

The items in the scale do not reflect many specific obsessions, compulsive rituals, or phobias, but cover such things as anxiety and dread, low self-confidence, doubts about one's competence, undue sensitivity, moodiness, and immobilization. The scale may also indicate withdrawal, poor concentration, agitation, denial of antisocial behavior, and poor physical health.

Relatively few persons with high **7** scores are ill enough for hospitalization; more often they are simply miserable with their symptoms, although occasionally they may be unable to carry on their ordinary occupations. The most disabling varieties of the high **7** pattern are characterized by a compulsive introspective attitude; the subject seems unable to let himself alone psychologically. An interesting aspect of the high **7** is that, although the persons are prone to be exacting and rigid in certain aspects of their behavior, they appear contrastingly opposite in others. This apparent inconsistency may be due to the fact that their standards are so high for all activities that they may fail to complete them, thus appearing to be sloppy or disorganized because they can't get things done to their satisfaction. Even among psychiatric patients high points on scale **7** are not particularly frequent, although they may be a little more frequent in psychiatric outpatient groups than in hospitalized groups. Guthrie found that medical patients with high points on **7** were characterized as prone to worry, anxious, fearful, and rigid. They presented problems centered around their hearts, with gastrointestinal and genitourinary complaints also. They showed extreme concern about their medical difficulty; they required many return visits and repeated reassurances. Depression was present, but even in the **72** codes it was less clearly manifested than were agitation and anxiety.

Black found that normal college girls with high points on **7** were described only as kind, dependent, quiet, and trustful. Drake and Oetting found that college counselees showed various anxiety symptoms with the particular symptoms related to the other elevations on the profile. Also noted were shyness and unresponsiveness in the interview. Mello and Guthrie found that college counselees with high points on **7** were characterized by obsessive-compulsive ruminations and morbid introspective trends. The problems of these students were centered about poor study habits, poor personal relations, and difficulty with authority figures.

Scale **7** appears to be most useful clinically in its relation to other scales, particularly **7** and **8**. Some of the two-digit code types discussed in Chapter 6 include the **27-72**'s, **78**, **87**'s, and **47-74**'s. In profiles dominated by other patterns, scale **7** generally reflects anxiety level; when the research scales are available **7** can be checked against the scale **A** score (see Chapter 5).

Hathaway and Meehl found that normal males with high **7**'s were described as sentimental, peaceable, good-tempered, verbal, individualistic, and dissatisfied. The normal women were described as sensitive, prone to worry, emotional, and high-strung. They were also seen as conscientious, intuitive, and having aesthetic interests. It has also been reported that college students with **7** peaks were particularly conscientious in reporting for psychological experiments and gave an unusually high number of uncertain judgments in the course of an experiment on a discrimination task.

Low scores on **7** are not too commonly seen and the description of the person probably depends largely on the rest of the profile. Hathaway and Meehl found that low **7** males were described as balanced, self-controlled, and independent; the females were described only as cheerful. Among college counselees a low point on **7** is rare but generally indicates good social adjustment.

Scale 8 (Sc)

Scale **8** measures the similarity of the subject's responses to those of patients who are characterized by bizarre and unusual thoughts or behavior. Scale **8** is the longest of the clinical scales and has very diverse content. Some of the items reflect the bizarre mentation, social alienation, peculiarities of perception, and feelings of persecution included in the classic description of schizophrenia. There are also items which deal with poor family relationships, lack of deep interests, concern with sexual matters, difficulties in concentration and impulse control, fears and worries, and the degree to which life is a strain.

Considering the diverse content of scale **8**, it is not surprising that adjective studies of various "normal" groups tend to give differing results. Hathaway and Meehl found that normal males with high **8** scores were described as prone to worry, self-dissatisfied, conscientious, good-tempered, versatile, verbal, and enthusiastic with wide interests and general aesthetic interests. They were also seen as frank, fair-minded, courageous, kind, sentimental, and peaceable. The high **8** women were seen as sensitive, high-strung, frank, courageous, kind, and modest. Among normals with high intelligence the high **8** score may also suggest creativity, originality, nonconformity, aesthetic interests, self-sufficiency, and responsiveness to inner stimuli. Among adolescents high scores on **8** are quite common. High **8** boys have been described by their teachers as followers, indifferent, unlikable, stubborn, hostile, lazy, and undependable. The female high **8**'s were called lazy, undependable, unlikable, erratic, unhappy, peppy, and scatterbrained. To some extent scale **8** probably reflects the confusion, alienation, and rebellion of adolescence. Here again high **8** with high intelligence may suggest creativity and productivity, but high **8** adolescents with low intelligence tend to show poor school performance and low socioeconomic level in later life.

Black found that normal college girls with high scores on **8** were described as apathetic, serious, seclusive, and secretive, but they were also seen as orderly, wise, clear-thinking, and adaptable. They were, in addition, described as worldly, sophisticated, humble, peaceable, and grateful. Mello and Guthrie found that college counselees with high points on **8** presented problems in peer relationships, group acceptance, sexual preoccupation, sexual confusion, and daydreaming. Drake and Oetting found that in male counselees high **8** scores tend to reflect many of the characteristics of scale **7** except that there were more indications of disorganized thinking or confusion. Among the female counselees the high **8** scores seemed to indicate more serious general disturbance with the high **8** seeming to emphasize the characteristics associated with the other scales in the pattern. When **0** and **8** were both high, nervousness, introverted behavior, and nonverbal behavior in the interview were suggested. When **2** and **8** were both high, depression, anxieties, study problems, and lack of skills with the opposite sex were noted. When **8** and **9** were both high, the counselee tended to be described as confused, restless, verbal, resistant in counseling, and requiring long-term counseling. When scale **0** was low, the high **8** score did not suggest as many problems.

Although high point **8** scores were relatively infrequent among medical patients, Guthrie reported on a small subgroup. These patients did not show clear-cut physical symptoms but presented a history of vague complaints that had been treated by a variety of regimes and suggested a long-standing stabilized hypochondriacal trend. They were described as disagreeable and their home life was severely disrupted by the poor control they maintained over their hostility. Generally they attributed their problems to trouble with their nerves but they did not benefit from simple reassurance and their response to treatment was poor.

Among psychiatric patients scale **8** needs to be evaluated in conjunction with the rest of the profile. The **48, 68, 78,** and **89** codes are of considerable interest and are discussed in Chapter 6. One should never diagnose schizophrenia on the basis of scale **8** only but in terms of the entire profile. Scales **0, Es,** and possibly **Cn** (see Chapter 5) are useful in evaluating scale **8** elevations also. Extreme elevations on **8** (T scores over 100) probably do not indicate schizophrenia; these scores are usually found in younger persons and may reflect confusion, alienation, or family or social problems, although occasionally a high score may be found in a person who appears very well adjusted.

Low **8** scores need to be evaluated in terms of the rest of the profile, but these persons are likely to be unimaginative, practical, conservative, and conventional but hard-working, responsible, and self-controlled.

Scale 9 (Ma)

Scale **9** appears to be primarily a measure of activity or energy level, but may indicate mood to some extent. At higher elevations **9** is suggestive of grandiosity, excitement, and flight of ideas. The item content of the scale is quite diverse; besides items suggesting grandiosity, excitement, and activity level there are also items relating to moral attitudes, home and family relationships, and physical and bodily matters.

Normal males with high **9** scores have been described as sociable, talkative, verbal, individualistic, impulsive, enthusiastic, adventurous, and curious. The normal females were similarly described although they were also called frank, courageous, and idealistic. For the Minnesota normative group, **9** on the profile was the most common high point and it tends to be a more frequent high point among normal groups than in clinical populations. The question of normality does not relate directly to the elevation of the score but rather to the quality of the overactivity. In many ways a relatively high **9** score is an asset to a person who wishes to be extrovertive and active. The borderline between normal and abnormal overactivity is a wide one and the determining point is often the individual's ability to finish the many things he is interested in and undertakes. He often gets so many things started that the whole effort slumps suddenly into a fiasco from which he emerges with a depression.

Gilberstadt and Duker have described a group of manic psychiatric patients whose profiles showed a peak score on **9** with no other scales over 70. They were all described as hyperactive, grandiose, and talkative. Usually these patients slept minimally and engaged in multiple projects and activities far into the night. Almost all had previous attacks of hypomania or depression. Some of these recurred at regular intervals and some appeared to be "anniversary reactions." Thinking and speech usually became bizarre during the acute hypomanic phase. Most of the patients flared up and became extremely belligerent when blocked or crossed in their activities. Frequently, patients feared being slowed down because they could anticipate a pending depression. In many patients there appeared to be an underlying obsessive-compulsive component, with behavior during non-illness phases being characterized by neatness, precision, and high standards. They usually showed normal job adjustment and generally normal life adjustment between illness phases.

Several studies have reported on college students with high points on **9**. Black reported that normal college women were described as enterprising, energetic, persevering, and idealistic, but also as awkward, infantile, boastful, show-offish, selfish, self-centered, and inflexible. Mello and Guthrie reported that college counselees were most frequently concerned with relationships stemming from problems in the local college setting. Drake and Oetting reported that high **9** with **0** coded low was associated with outgoing, verbal, and socially skilled behavior. Among the males, when **0** was not low it was associated with aggressive behavior. The girls with high **9** and low **5** scores showed symptoms of physical exhaustion.

5

The Research Scales

The basic concept of the MMPI assumes that among the 550 items there are groupings of items that can form an indefinite number of additional scales for special purposes. Over 450 scales and subscales have been developed thus far, but these scales vary considerably in development, standardization, validation, range of application, and supplementary information available. At this time some scoring systems such as the National Computer Systems* provide routine scoring of twelve additional scales when all the MMPI items are administered. These have been scored according to norms of the original MMPI standardization group, so that these scales have a common frame of reference with respect to each other as well as to the clinical scales. These twelve scales are discussed briefly in this chapter for those people who have the scores on them regularly available and would like some idea of their possible use and interpretation. Of these scales the **Lb** and **Ca** scales should probably be limited in use to patients with certain special medical problems, but the other scales may be of some interest for various groups.

Si (0) Scale

The **Si** scale has become so popular that it is regarded by many as the tenth clinical scale and is coded as **0** in the Welsh coding system, even though its primary usefulness has been with normal subjects, particularly in the guidance and counseling fields. Developed originally

*NCS, 4401 West 76th Street, Minneapolis, Minn. 55435.

on female college students with the Minnesota T-S-E inventory (see Welsh and Dahlstrom, 1956, Article 19) used as a criterion, the scale has been demonstrated by other studies to measure the tendency toward social introversion or avoidance of social contacts with others. Lower scores indicate a tendency toward extroversion or a preference for social activities and associations with others.

Some of the items in the scale describe the person's uneasiness in social situations or in dealings with others; some cover a variety of special sensitivities, insecurities, and worries. Still other items deny many impulses, temptations, and mental aberrations, and some items indicate conservative tendencies and self-depreciation. A factor analysis of the scale suggests six components: inferiority-discomfort, lack of affiliation, low social excitement, sensitivity, interpersonal trust, and physical somatic concern. High scores on this scale can be composed largely of the social isolation components or the maladjustment and self-depreciation components (or both).

Hathaway and Meehl (1952) found that there was an important sex difference in the degree to which peers were able to characterize normal persons with this scale elevated. The men were described only as modest; perhaps the personality pattern of these men served to keep the raters from knowing them well enough to describe them more fully. The women, however, were seen as modest, shy, self-effacing, and sensitive. There were indications of emotional warmth in the use of adjectives like kind, affectionate, softhearted, and sentimental, and although called high-strung, they were also seen as natural, serious, and having home and family interests. Hathaway and Meehl found that low-scoring males were seen as versatile and sociable in the sense of mixing well. The women were described by their acquaintances as sociable, enthusiastic, talkative, assertive, and adventurous.

Drake and Oetting (1959) found that 0 in male college counselees was associated with various introvertive characteristics, especially shyness, social insecurity, and social withdrawal. When scales 2 and 0 were both coded high, the pattern was likely to be associated with a lack of social skills as well as introversion and feelings of social insecurity. When scales 7 and 0 were both coded high the problem was likely to be more serious and extensive; the counselee was likely to be depressed, to be indecisive, to have conflict with his mother, and to be shy in the interview situation. A low coding of scale 0 was indicative of an adequate social adjustment, even in patterns usually associated with somewhat serious problems. There is a tempering of the problems often associated with the scales making up the rest of the pattern.

The high 0 females in the counseling study were rated similarly to the men; they were also described as lacking skill with the opposite sex. This latter difficulty was noted particularly when scale 2 was coded high with scale 0. When scale 6 was paired high with scale 0, the subjects were described as having feelings of inferiority in regard to some physical feature. When scale 7 was coded high with scale 0, it seemed related to the same type of problems but also to a more generalized feeling of insecurity. Both scale 8 and scale 0 coded high suggested not only shyness but problems in communicating with the counselor as well; these subjects tended to be shy in the interview, unable to talk well to the counselor, and nervous. When scale 0 was coded low for females it appeared to indicate a good general adjustment including freedom from parental conflicts. These subjects were also seen as oriented more toward marriage than girls with high codes and lacking in academic motivation.

Studies of adolescents also suggest that high 0 is indicative of lack of social activity as well as feelings of social inadequacy. The low scores suggested social participation and confidence. The high scores were noted more frequently in boys and girls from farms, whereas low 0 suggested urban residence and high socioeconomic status. The high 0's showed good school conduct and rarely were delinquent or school dropouts or had other kinds of emotional problems. The low 0's were seen as having high ability but not high academic achievement; they seldom dropped out of school altogether, however. Low 0 scores were not often associated with delinquency either.

Few research data are available on clinical groups for the 0 scale but clinical experience suggests that this can be a valuable adjunct in use with scales 2, 7, and 8 to indicate the degree of social withdrawal or shyness related to these scale elevations.

Studies of couples seen for marriage counseling (see Arnold, 1970) suggest that 0 is an important factor in marital conflict when the scores of the pair differ by more than 20 T points. This is noted particularly when the wife has an **0** score higher than her husband's. In marriage conflicts there is also some tendency for either a low **9** score or a low **Es** score to be associated with a high **0** in one of the pair, and a high **9** or a high **Es** with a low **0** in the other person. The high **9**, low **0** is known as the "socializer" pattern and the low **9**, high **0** is known as the "nonsocializer" pattern. We may speculate that the energetic outgoingness of one spouse who revels in social interaction outside the home has a life-style that is potentially disruptive when mated with a partner who is less energetic and also less inclined to interact with others than the spouse.

A and R Scales

Both the **A** and the **R** scales were developed by Welsh from various factor analytic studies that have been done on the MMPI (see Welsh and Dahlstrom, 1956, Article 29). These scales were developed and intended to be used together, so this section will discuss them together as well as separately.

The **A** scale was developed (by a variant of the internal consistency method) as a relatively pure measure of the first factor found in most factor analysis study. It can be considered to be measuring anxiety or general maladjustment. The items seem to relate to thinking difficulties, anxiety and worry, unhappiness, guilt, loneliness, lack of energy and pessimism, and personal sensitivity. The **A** scale is highly correlated with scales **7, 8,** and **2** as well as negatively with **K.**

The **R** scale is a measure of the second factor found in most factor analytic studies. The item content is much more diverse than the **A** scale but the scale seems to be measuring the tendency to use the various mechanisms of repression, denial, and rationalization as well as a lack of self-insight. Some researchers have viewed **R** as a measure of introversion rather than repression, however.

Welsh has done considerable research comparing various **A** and **R** combinations with various code and profile patterns as well as diagnostic groups. The **A** and **R** scores are obviously useful tools in analyzing profile patterns, and in conjunction with the other scores on the MMPI have considerable utility in their own right.

The Es (Ego Strength) Scale

The **Es** scale was originally developed (see Welsh and Dahlstrom, 1956, Article 26) to predict favorable response to psychotherapy, but in addition it appears to measure a more general personality variable or variables related to psychological ideas about "ego strength." This scale includes items concerning physical functioning, stability, psychasthenia, seclusiveness, religious attitudes, moral attitudes, sense of reality, personal adequacy, ability to cope, phobias, and infantile anxieties.

On the basis of item content, the person with a high **Es** score might be expected to have some of the following characteristics: good physical functioning; spontaneity, the ability to share emotional experiences; conventional church membership, but not fundamentalistic or dogmatic in religious beliefs; permissive morality; good contact with reality; feelings of personal adequacy and vitality; physical courage and lack of fear.

The low-scoring **Es** person is likely to show the opposite of these traits, or a tendency toward some of the following qualities: many and chronic physical ailments; broodiness, inhibition, a strong need for emotional seclusion, worrisomeness; intense religious experience, belief in prayer, miracles, and literal interpretation of the Bible; repressive and punitive morality; dissociation and ego alienation; confusion, submissiveness, chronic fatigue; phobias and infantile anxieties.

The **Es** scale has been evaluated as a measure of control over hostility by Barron (see Welsh and Dahlstrom, 1956, Article 64). In general, high scorers on **Es** were effective and healthy in the management they exercised over aggressive feelings and impulses. However, Barron found that more accurate predictions could be made when certain childhood experiences of a subject were taken into consideration along with the **Es** score. That is, a high scorer on **Es** may show poor control over hostility, along with a general egoism, if he has had childhood experiences characterized by friction in the home, poor relationships with his parents, or a mother lacking in emotional warmth. Low scorers on **Es** did not present a consistent picture in the way they handled hostility but were generally submissive, rigid, and unadaptive in several emotional areas. Thus, the **Es** scale seems to provide information about style of behavior, but the intensity of impulse to aggression must come from some other personality dimension.

The Es scale correlates positively with vitality, drive, self-confidence, poise, breadth of interest, intellectual efficiency, and general intelligence as measured by a variety of tests.

Cross-validation studies in various psychiatric situations, both inpatient and outpatient, tend to substantiate the usefulness of the Es scale in predicting response to psychotherapy. A T score of 50 has been typically used as a cutting point, but this might not be as effective as another in some settings. In several studies the Es score has been noted to rise following a successful treatment outcome. One might also expect the Es to be useful in predicting reaction to stress whether induced by the external environment or produced physiologically by illness or chemotherapy. The Es scale also gives some information about the current integration of the personality, and may be helpful in diagnosing schizophrenia in conjunction with scales 8 and 0.

In Arnold's (1970) study of marriage problems he found that marital conflict was more likely to occur if the Es scores for both husband and wife were below 50 or if a difference of more than 15 points occurred between the two scores. Contrary to expectation the presence of both Es scores over 65 did not indicate marital conflict.

The Lb (Low Back Pain) Scale

The low back pain scale, Lb (Hanvik, 1949; see also Welsh and Dahlstrom, 1956, Article 55), consists of 25 MMPI items which differentiated between patients with low back pain diagnosed to be due to a protruding intervertebral disc (the "organics") and patients whose low back pain had not been diagnosed as resulting from an organic disease (the "functionals"). Comparisons of the MMPI profiles for the two groups showed the mean profiles for the "functionals" to be characterized by a conversion V pattern (see the section on 13-31 codes) with a secondary peak on scale 7. The mean "organic" profile was characterized by scales 1, 2, and 3 nearly equal and slightly higher than the rest of the profile. The two groups differed most on scales 1 and 3, with the "functionals" also significantly higher than the "organics" on **2, 4, 7,** and **8.** Although 10 of the **Lb** items are also on scales **1** and **3,** the content of the scales is fairly diverse and 11 of the items do not appear on any clinical scale. The **Lb** scale correlates significantly with scales **1, 3, 4,** and **K,** but the correlations are low enough to justify using the **Lb** scale in addition to the MMPI profile in cases with low back pain.

In using the **Lb** scale in clinical practice, a high score would be interpreted as suggestive of "functional" low back pain, whereas a low score would suggest "organic" low back pain. In Hanvik's total group of 100 cases a cutting line between raw scores of 10 and 11 misclassified only 12 cases and these were within 5 raw score points or less of the cutting score. Clinically, it is probably better to use a T score of 70 (Hathaway and Briggs norms, 1957) or higher to identify functional cases.

In practice it is well to remember that a person with a high **Lb** score may still have organic pathology, since neurosis does not protect one from physical damage. On the other hand, considerable caution should be exercised before performing any radical procedures on high **Lb** patients. As Hanvik suggests, the same attributes that lead to functional complaints may serve to complicate recovery after surgery for bona fide structural defects. Low **Lb** score patients should be studied carefully, however, before ruling out organic disease.

Although clinicians occasionally try to use the **Lb** score in other kinds of functional versus organic decisions, there is no research evidence to indicate that this is justifiable, and considerable caution and restraint would be indicated in using this scale with conditions other than low back pain.

The Ca (Caudality) Scale

The **Ca** scale was developed to assist in locating focal brain damage (see Welsh and Dahlstrom, 1956, Article 25). It was found in comparing profiles of subjects with localized brain damage that persons with parietal damage had elevations on scales **2** and **7,** whereas those with frontal damage had rather flat profiles with an elevation on **8.** The temporal cases were most like the parietal cases except for a secondary spike on scale **8.**

The **Ca** scale consists of 37 items which discriminate between cases with frontal and with parietal brain damage. The items primarily suggest anxiety, depression, guilt, introversion, feelings of inadequacy, worry about the future, and somatic concern. Low scores suggest frontal damage and high scores nonfrontal damage. If a cutting score of 11 raw score points (T score = 49) is used for a population with frontal and parietal cases equal, only about 22 percent are misclassified. (The possibility of error would be greater in populations with unequal proportions.) In view of this the **Ca** scale cannot be used alone for localizing brain damage but it is a valuable adjunct to other clinical data. The previous personality of the patient is probably an important factor in the errors made by the scale. For example, an obsessive-compulsive person who is extremely anxious and depressed, and who has a therapeutically unsuccessful frontal lobotomy, would probably still receive a high **Ca** score. It should also be pointed out that the **Ca** scale cannot be used for diagnosing brain damage, but only to help in localizing it when it has already been diagnosed or indicated by other methods.

Dy (Dependency) Scale

The **Dy** scale is a judgmentally derived scale developed by Navran (1954). He used both the consensus of judges who rated the suitability of the items for measuring direct or manifest dependency and an internal consistency analysis of the items for final inclusion in the scale. He reported that this scale differentiated between normals and psychiatric cases although there is no evidence that these differences are attributable solely to dependency. There is some evidence that this scale indicates ulcer patients are somewhat more dependent than normals.

Do (Social Dominance) Scale

Gough, McClosky, and Meehl (see Welsh and Dahlstrom, 1956, Article 24) derived the **Do** scale from groups of high school and college students nominated by their peers as most dominant and least dominant. Dominance was considered to be expressed by social initiative, leadership ability, persistence, and strong and forceful actions. The items on the scale suggest that the more dominant person has more poise, self-assurance, and self-confidence. He appears to have resoluteness, optimism, resourcefulness, and efficiency. He also appears to have perseverance, a "dutiful" sense of morality, and deep-seated seriousness.

Re (Social Responsibility) Scale

The **Re** scale was developed by Gough, McClosky, and Meehl (1952) as a scale of social responsibility, indicated by willingness to take the consequences of one's own behavior and by trustworthiness, dependability, and a sense of obligation to the group. The item selection for this scale was based upon subjects identified by peer nominations among high school students and college student organizations. This scale also stood up well in new groups reflecting assessment staff rating of responsibility and character integration, nominations for responsibility and for good school citizenship, school disciplinary problems, and self-rating on concern for group activities. High **Re** scores were also noted to be significant among a sample of happily married couples (Arnold, 1970).

Pr (Prejudice) Scale

The **Pr** scale was developed by Gough (see Welsh and Dahlstrom, 1956, Article 23) as a measure of anti-Semitic prejudice using the Levinson-Sanford anti-Semitism scale for selecting criterion groups of high school students high and low in prejudice. Item analysis of the scale suggests that several factors are typical of prejudiced students. One factor is anti-intellectuality; a second is a sense of pessimism and lack of hope and confidence in the future. The prejudiced students also seem to show cynicism, distrust, doubt, suspicion, misanthropy, querulousness, a hostile and bitter outlook and repining, grumbling, and discontented evaluation of their current status. They show as well a rigid, dogmatic style of thinking, lack of poise and assurance, perplexity, fearfulness, and feelings of estrangement and isolation. There has been some research to indicate that the **Pr** scale is correlated positively with other scales such as the California E-F scale, the California F scale, and the Purdue Attitude Scale toward Jews. The **Pr** scale is also positively correlated with Maslow's Security-Insecurity Inventory suggesting that prejudiced persons are likely to be insecure. High **Pr** scorers have also been reported as prudish, religious, and rigid.

Clinical impression suggests that in the 1970s, at least with university students and graduate students, the scale operates in a different way: very low scores are common (T < 40). Score distributions on blacks, chicanos, and American Indians have not been reported, nor have distributions on ethnic enclaves. Low scores may represent adherence to a formal, liberal political position and the personality correlates of high scores may not be as dependable as they were in earlier reports.

St (Socioeconomic Status) Scale

Gough (see Welsh and Dahlstrom, 1956, Article 21) developed the **St** scale on a group of high school students who had been divided into high- and low-status groups by means of the Sims Score Card (Sims, 1927) ratings on their families. It was also correlated with the American Home Scale, another measure of socioeconomic status. The items on the scale can be divided into five general groups: literary and aesthetic attitudes; social poise, security, confidence in self and others; denial of fears and anxieties; "broadminded," "emancipated," and "frank" attitudes toward moral, religious, and sexual matters; and positive, dogmatic, and self-righteous opinions. Again, social changes in the psychological significance of socioeconomic status in the last quarter century may alter the meaning of elevations in some groups and lessen the scale's clinical usefulness.

Cn (Control) Scale

Cuadra (see Welsh and Dahlstrom, 1956, Article 27) developed the **Cn** scale as a measure of the need for hospitalization. The items were those that discriminated between two groups matched on the basis of MMPI profiles, age, and sex but differing in the need for inpatient hospital treatment. A low score on the scale indicates that the person is more like the hospitalization group whereas a high score would indicate greater personality control. The items in the scale suggest that the high-scoring person might be described as rather sophisticated, realistic, somewhat impatient with naive, overly moralistic, and opinionated persons, but quite aware of his own weaknesses and inwardly sensitive to social criticism. A person answering in the opposite direction would be described as fairly conventional, moralistic, and disinclined to experiment with and explore the environment about him. In other words, high scorers seem to depend more on internal controls and self-direction. Low scorers depend more on social conventions, moralistic rules, and stable environments.

6

Two-Digit Codes

In recent years there have appeared a number of "cookbooks" for MMPI interpretation such as Gilberstadt and Duker's (1965) or Marks and Seeman's (1963), as well as various kinds of computer interpretation services, but the two-digit codes (numbers for the two highest scales) remain an indispensable aid in clinical interpretation. If codes are classified by the first two digits, disregarding their order, there are 28 theoretically possible code types (excluding noncoded and single-digit cases and scales 5 and 0). Fortunately, some of these combinations occur more frequently than others, so that it is possible to deal with the great majority of profiles under a few common types. The relative frequency of these code types in various groups is itself of considerable interest and the tables in the clinical *Atlas* (Hathaway and Meehl, 1951a) and the *Handbook*, volume I (Dahlstrom, Welsh, and Dahlstrom, 1972), are worth careful study.

This chapter presents material derived from many sources and research studies; most of this material is also summarized in volume I of the *Handbook*. Although some of the studies present quite differing results, for some of the code types there appears to be a core of common symptoms of personality traits whatever the populations used. Thus while the test user must be very familiar with the particular population with which he is working, he may be able to use material drawn from other groups as well. Absolute scale elevation and the presence or absence of other scales are not usually indicated in these research reports, but such factors should also be considered in using the material presented in this chapter.

The material reported from Halbower (1955), Gilberstadt and Duker, and Marks and Seeman does not represent all cases with the respective codes but only those with more closely defined profile characteristics. The definitions of these profile types are given in the *Handbook* or the respective references. The material is presented here in order to amplify the information on the two-digit codes, but it must be recognized that some caution is needed in use of the data. Halbower and Gilberstadt and Duker dealt with male Veterans Administration psychiatric inpatients, whereas Marks and Seeman presented both male and female cases from both inpatient and outpatient psychiatric settings in a large medical center. Other sources are Hathaway and Meehl (1952), Guthrie (1949), Drake (1954, 1956), Black (1953), Welsh and Sullivan (1952), Arnold (1970), Sines (1966), Persons and Marks (1971), Drake and Oetting (1959), and Forsyth and Smith (1967).

12 and 21 Codes

The psychiatric patients with **12** and **21** codes studied by Hathaway and Meehl had, in the majority of cases, pain, regardless of formal diagnosis. Depression, irritability, shyness, seclusiveness, and somatic concern as distinguished from conversion were found also. These people were anxious, worried, or concerned about the state of their bodies. This code is much more frequent among psychiatric patients than among normal groups. Two-thirds of the patients in the psychiatric group study received a formal diagnosis of psychoneurosis, chiefly somatic (hypochondriasis, hysteria) and some "mixed." The remaining third were split between schizophrenia and manic-depression. Psychopathic personality and conduct disorders were rare.

In Guthrie's medical group study, the **12**'s were described with the **13**'s. These patients presented numerous complaints with a strong emphasis on abdominal distress and backaches. There was little demonstrable physical pathology. Their distress appeared to be only moderate but their histories showed a high frequency of visits to doctors over a protracted period of time with symptomatic relief usually short-lived. Little could be learned concerning the emotional factors in the background of these patients, for they concentrated on their aches and pains and had relatively little insight about their personal adjustment. The internist working with these patients had the impression that they, more than any other group, had learned to live with and to use their complaints to such an extent that they were difficult to treat. Few showed marked changes for better or worse over periods of several years but there were brief reductions of symptoms over short periods of a month or more. The **12** group reported more feelings of anxiety and tension than the **13** group. The differences between the men and women with **12** and **13** codes are in accord with a trend that appeared in all Guthrie's groups; the men placed less emphasis on their emotional difficulties and more on their physical symptoms. This is probably a function of our culture in which it is more acceptable for women to admit their worries and fears than it is for men. Item analyses show that the **12**'s and **13**'s obtained their elevated scores primarily from enumeration of their symptoms. They pictured themselves in terms of their symptoms and did not admit with significant frequency any items which related to emotional problems.

Guthrie's medical group study described the **21**'s and **23**'s together. The male patients of this group complained of one or the other of two symptoms: marked epigastric distress or tension and depression. Nothing was found in their profiles to differentiate these two groups. In contrast to the **12**'s and **13**'s there was for these patients a more marked concentration of symptoms in the upper gastrointestinal tract with few who presented multiple aches and pains. The **21**'s and **23**'s resembled the ulcer syndrome described by Alexander (1934): they were competitive and industrious but immature and dependent. Though they dreaded increased responsibilities they sought promotions in their jobs. In spite of their difficulties they had maintained their normal level of efficiency. Very few of these patients had demonstrable physical pathology. When no pathology was found, about half of them did not return for further treatment. There were no data to explain whether they responded favorably to reassurance or went to other physicians who would not emphasize the emotional etiology of their disorders.

Analysis of the items characteristic of this group suggests such persons suffer from loss of self-confidence, lack of efficiency, brooding, a subtle rigidity of outlook, sensitiveness, and inability to feel comfortable with people. There were items for the **21**'s which told of poor health and of aches and pains. No items of this sort appeared in the **23** results.

Gilberstadt and Duker have reported on three subgroups, the **123**'s, **1234**'s, and **1237**'s, and Marks and Seeman included the **213**'s with the **231**'s. The cardinal features of the **123** type included somatic symptoms, usually of autonomic nervous system origin. These patients tended to react to emotion-producing life stresses with physiological symptoms rather than the usual affect. They reportedly lacked aggressiveness and sexual drive, but had stable work and marital adjustment. They also complained of being irritable, nervous, weak, tired, fatigued, and worrying.

Halbower has also reported on a subgroup of **123** patients in a VA Mental Hygiene Clinic. These patients presented themselves as organically ill and manifested either a somatization reaction or other psychophysiological reaction. These patients showed a hypochondriacal picture in which complaints of pain, easy fatiguability, and weariness were prominent. They were also described as hypersensitive and they overevaluated minor dysfunctions.

The **1234** group had as their most frequent symptom severe alcoholism. Many of them had stomach distress, ulcers, or gastrectomies. Other somatic complaints included headaches, backaches, blackouts, and shoulder pain. Symptoms of depression such as insomnia, anorexia, and suicidal attempts or intentions were frequent. Also noted were shyness, irritability, worrying, tension, low frustration tolerance, rage reactions, impulsiveness, and authority problems. Many of their symptoms may be a result of their alcoholism.

The **1237**'s are similar to the **123**'s but differ in showing a higher frequency of anxiety, tension, back pain, chest pain, dependency, and inadequacy. They may have actual organic illnesses as well as hypochondriacal fixations. They're described as weak, fearful, highly inadequate. They may regress and become unable to work or to take ordinary stresses or simple, everyday responsibilities.

13 and 31 Codes

The **13** and **31** code type has become known as the conversion V, with scale **2** falling below the two somatic variables on the profile. In the majority of these cases, two things appeared: pain and some symptoms involving eating. Other kinds of conversion also occurred. The eating problem appeared as actual anorexia or hysterical vomiting, or the person complained of discomfort after eating or when he ate too much. Also the **13**'s and **31**'s tended to complain of pain in different places than the **12**'s and **21**'s. They had pain in the head very commonly and in the arms, back, legs, eyes, neck, etc., whereas the **12**'s and **21**'s tended to have pain in the trunk, especially the lower bowel and the like. When the **31** and **13** cases did have inner pain, it occurred higher up in the body cavity, for example, precordial pain.

A sizable minority of the **31** and **13** cases were described as sociable and extroverted. This socially oriented hysterical personality characterizes many people with conversion symptoms, although not all by any means. It is, however, much more frequent among persons with conversion symptoms than among those who are hypochondriacal, obsessive, and anxious. Also marked in a sizable minority was objection to psychiatric study. They came into the hospital for their sore back; now they were being processed for this "mind" business, and they did not like it a bit.

This code is second most frequent for the psychiatric population. The overwhelming majority of these cases were neurotics, the very small proportion of psychotics and psychopaths being atypical of their class. This is more characteristically a feminine than a masculine configuration and in men suggests a socially oriented, passively dependent person who uses somatization to achieve neurotic ends.

The **13**'s in Guthrie's medical group have been discussed already (see **12**'s) and they differ very little from the **31**'s. The complaints of the **31**'s were of the sort that arise during protracted periods of mild tension. They include headaches, backaches, pains in the chest, and abdominal distress. Conversion hysteria was exceedingly rare in Guthrie's group so that it is not surprising that there was only one instance of it in this subgroup. Few of these patients were incapacitated by their symptoms. They appeared on interview to have a lengthy history of insecurity and immaturity and a tendency to develop symptoms when stresses increased. In contrast to those whose highest scale was **2**, these patients placed little stress on the discomforts of their current emotional state, and in contrast to those whose highest scale was **1**, their physical complaints were more specific and the disorders they presented were of a somewhat more episodic nature. They differed significantly from the rest of the subjects in the medical group on items which told of aches and pains and on subtle items suggesting a hysterical lack of self-criticism.

Black's **13-31** college girls tend to be uncritical of themselves and show a generally impunitive view of others, the world, and themselves. Their peers, however, describe them as selfish and self-centered with many physical complaints. Girls seen in college counseling centers (Drake and Oetting) seemed to be extroverted, socially outgoing, and able to verbalize their difficulties easily. They reported many conflicts centering around their parents and showed poor academic motivation. They complained about blocking and tightening up in examinations. College boys seen in counseling were aggressive in the initial interview. They insisted on knowing results of their tests and sought definitive answers from the counselor. They appeared socially skillful and confident, were fluent and expressive in the interview, and related well to the counselor. They appeared free of tensions, restlessness, nervousness, and other signs of disturbance. They were frequently seen only once, without returns to the center.

Halbower's group of VA patients manifested somatization or psychophysiological reactions and were seen as gaining from these symptoms by getting out of painful or stressful situations. They were characterized as very self-centered, selfish, dependent, and demanding in their personal relationships. They tended to use mechanisms such as rationalization, blaming others, projection, and acting out. They appeared emotionally labile, easily stimulated, and poorly controlled emotionally.

Marks and Seeman reported on a group of females with this code who showed primarily conversion reactions or psychophysiological disorders. They tended to have many somatic complaints including fatigue, weakness, back pain, headache, nausea, vomiting, numbness, dizziness and ulcers. Many of them were anxious, depressed, tense, and complained of insomnia or sleep disturbance. They tended to have inner conflicts about emotional dependency and an exaggerated need for affection. Gilberstadt and Duker reported on four subgroups of the **13**'s: **137**'s, **132**'s, **138**'s, and **139**'s.

The **132**'s were similar to other **13** groups. They were diagnosed as conversion reaction with depression, or psychophysiological reactions, or anxiety reactions. They were described as hysteroid, passive-dependent, sociable, extroverted, and well liked until they showed irritability and symptoms of reactive depression. Their physical complaints included anorexia, nausea, vomiting, back pain, chest pain, and headaches, weakness, tiredness, and fatigue.

The **137**'s differed from the other **13**'s primarily in their high level of anxiety; they were frequently diagnosed as anxiety reaction, phobic reactions, or anxiety hysteria. In addition they complained of depression, fearfulness, nervousness, and tension. They also showed physical complaints such as anorexia, nausea, vomiting, cardiac complaints, shortness of breath, respiratory problems, epigastric problems, headache, leg or knee pains, weakness, tiredness, and fatigue. They had various vocational and financial problems and were usually childish, passive-dependent, rigid, and poor adapters to environmental changes.

The **138**'s tended to show symptoms of schizophrenic thinking disturbances such as blocking, ambivalence, religiosity, and paranoid ideas. Conversion symptoms and hypochondriacal features which apparently defended against schizophrenic outbreaks were common. They were also described as agitated, compulsive, depressed, suicidal, heavy drinkers, emotionally flat, suspicious, jealous, and paranoid. They showed bizarre sexual preoccupations, compulsions and fears regarding homosexuality, but appeared to deny psychosexual passivity by seeking masculine occupation. Drinking resulted in regressive psychotic behavior. Gilberstadt and Duker felt that they were pseudoneurotic or chronic schizophrenic.

The **139**'s were frequently associated with chronic organic illness, particularly the chronic brain syndrome. In the chronic brain syndrome they showed temper outbursts and increasing irritation until they became combative and destructive. Others complained of abdominal pain, back pain, blindness or eye problems, headaches, loss of appetite, numbness, tremor, and loss of consciousness. They showed comparatively little intellectual deterioration or disturbance of sensory motor functions, however.

In evaluating **13** and **31** codes found in nonmedical or nonpsychiatric settings, the **K** score and raw score on **1** should be rechecked. Some persons with **31** profiles may obtain the **1** score almost entirely on the basis of **K** correction, but if the raw score on **1** is over 10, then one would look for some neurotic symptoms. "Normal" subjects with conversion V's below 70 have been characterized as cheerful, outgoing, sociable people who tend to be optimistic and look on the bright side of everything. Because of their repressive tendencies they may appear flighty and immature at times. Although under stress they may develop physical symptoms, ordinarily they will present themselves as exceedingly normal, responsible, helpful, and sympathetic.

14 and 41 Codes

These codes seem to be relatively rare in both normal and clinical groups, although it is possible for scales **1** and **4** to be the highest when a number of the clinical scales are elevated. In a psychiatric population they may appear to be paranoid. Guthrie noted a small group of medical patients with **41** codes. These patients seemed to be clearly hypochondriacal with severe symptoms, there being little clear evidence of asocial behavior. They presented problems that were very resistant to treatment.

23 and 32 Codes

In the psychiatric group study of Hathaway and Meehl, results on the **23** and **32** codes were reported for the women only. The majority showed depression, and a minority complained of weakness, apathy, agitation, or tenseness. Among women this code was much more common in the psychiatric group than in normal groups. Diagnostically, these cases were about equally likely to be psychotic (manic-depressive depression and involutionals — almost never schizophrenic or paranoid states, although the **23** code is the common code for patients diagnosed paranoid) or psychoneurotic (scattered over subtypes, although conversion hysteria was rare). As with the preceding group, psychopathy was contraindicated by this code type.

Guthrie's **23** group was described with the **21**'s. They differed in items indicating inefficiency and inadequacy rather than somatic symptoms. They described themselves as unable to do things or even to start them. They have difficulties expressing their feelings, are bottled up, and filled with self-doubts and insecurities. They lack interest or involvement in things and feel constantly fatigued and exhausted, nervous and inadequate much of the time. The women were termed inadequate and immature. They frequently showed family or marital maladjustment but divorce was rarely reported for these women. Their unhappiness was chronic and prolonged but they showed little pressure to seek help, apparently tolerating unhappiness more than other persons and operating at a lower level of efficiency for long periods of time.

Like the **23**'s, the **32** group was found difficult to report on because fewer than half of them returned for further treatment following the administration of the test. And again there was no way to discover whether they changed physicians to avoid discussing their personal adjustment. Those who continued contacts showed a history of changing symptoms, neither increasing nor decreasing in severity. Although scale **2** was elevated, there was little evidence of depressive trends. The item analysis produced a small number of items telling of concern for their health. The remaining items were of the Hy-subtle variety (see page 28 above for a discussion of Hy-subtle) which give a picture of an individual who verbally conforms strictly to approved behavior patterns. The **32**'s denied unacceptable impulses and ideas and any feeling of social inadequacy. These data together with those obtained from interviews suggest an insightless, nonintrospective person who is very resistant to psychotherapy.

Marks and Seeman reported on a group of **231**'s and **213**'s combined. This group showed a combination of depressive and somatic symptoms including anxiety, tension, headache, insomnia, fatigue, anorexia, nausea and vomiting, weight loss, cardiac symptoms, chest pain, and alcoholism. They showed conflicts about self-assertion, basic insecurity, need for attention, and intropunitiveness.

24 and 42 Codes

This code type has not been reported very extensively in the literature. Guthrie found a small subgroup of medical patients with this profile. The **24**'s showed depressive patterns, usually associated with agitation and restlessness. Some men with this pattern reported severe epigastric distress, with positive evidence on X-ray of ulcerative conditions. Some of these patients, particularly with scale **2** and several other scales at a primed level, were clearly psychotic. Only one case with **24** had a well-established history of alcoholism and drug addiction. There were some other indications of psychopathic backgrounds in the group, however. At the time of testing these patients appared to be seriously seeking help from the physician and treatment was moderately successful. Guthrie reported that the **42**'s showed physical symptoms in only half of the cases. They impressed the internist as being severely psychoneurotic with psychopathic features, although some of the women with gross elevations were considered prepsychotic. Alcoholism and peptic ulcers were noteworthy in the small group of **42** men. There was little evidence of any response to treatment on the part of these patients.

Although this profile has often been called the "psychopath in trouble" type, in the belief that the elevation of **2** is simply due to current situational pressures, these people seem to be clearly different from the spike **4**'s, **49**'s, etc. In some cases the **4** probably represents hostility and resentment regarding some current situational problem and the **2** is the basic personality feature. When both scales in this high-point pair are grossly elevated (over 85) the pattern is associated with psychotic or prepsychotic behavior, and suicide is a serious possibility. A **24** is observed fairly frequently in aged people where it does not suggest antisocial acting out. The elevation on **4** represents a pervasive lack of satisfaction and the **2** reflects general and often chronic unhappiness.

Marks and Seeman included the **247**'s with **274**'s and **472**'s. This group is discussed here in the section on **27** and **72**'s. It seems to be characterized mainly by the **27** kind of symptoms with the **4** represented mainly by passive-aggressive traits.

The **24** and **42** codes are more common among marriage counselees than among normal or psychiatric populations and are somewhat more common for men than women. They seem to reflect the frustration and depression in an individual who feels "trapped" or inconvenienced at not getting his own way in the marriage. Such a person is typically egocentric and immature, has a low tolerance for frustration, and seems unable to engage in the cooperative "give and take" aspects of the relationship. He is apt to vacillate between self-pity and projected blame in trying to control the relationship with his mate, but only rarely faces up to his own deficiencies in the marital relationship or makes any concerted effort to modify his own behavior. When he does, it is begrudgingly and what admissions of culpability or changes are forthcoming are not ego-syntonic to him. Clinically, this pattern occasionally seems to occur in the profile of a passive-dependent male, and is accompanied by an elevated scale **5**. Such a person, typically, expresses a great deal of self-pity and whiningly deplores his wife's deficiencies as a wife and mother, a role she has typically played according to his specifications for a number of years until tiring of the charade. While sometimes a rigid set of traditional values are invoked in his denunciation, one gets the distinct impression that they represent not so much an internalized and deeply cherished value system to him as a set of specifications designed to make life easier for him, and to fulfill his own expectations in the marital relationship. Often, too, such an individual has a doting mother in his background and his wife tends to feel more like a mother than a wife.

26 and 62 Codes

Guthrie found that among the **26**'s the personality problems of this group stand out more prominently than physical distress. A subgroup of his subjects with this code showed allergies or obesity, or complained of diffuse pains. These patients showed strong evidence of paranoid trends; some of them were in early phases of a psychosis. Sensitivity, resentfulness, and aggressiveness were marked. These patients as a group were typically fatigued, resentful, hostile, and depressed. Their conditions were chronic and stabilized; they showed little change from one visit to another. The **62**'s also seemed depressed, worried, and concerned over their physical difficulties, with a strong underlying feeling of hostility. They had long histories of interpersonal difficulties and rejection of close associations, their hostilities seemingly handicapping them significantly in social skills. Such patients were severely neurotic, with a subgroup of them appearing actually prepsychotic. Guthrie also noted that they tended to be more disturbed than their moderate elevations on the MMPI would indicate. The height of the **F** scale, however, did seem to be proportional to the severity of their disturbance.

27 and 72 Codes

The majority of Hathaway and Meehl's psychiatric patients with **27** and **72** were depressed; they showed anxiety, insomnia, and undue sensitiveness and they were described as tense or nervous. This code group was the largest for the psychiatric population, and psychosis was slightly more frequent than neurosis. The commonest psychotic diagnosis for these cases was depression (manic-depressive or involutional; schizophrenia occurred but was rare). The modal neurotic diagnosis in both sexes was reactive depression with obsessive-compulsive neurosis running close behind. Mixed neurosis and hypochondriasis were unlikely and conversion hysteria was definitely contraindicated. Psychopathy was also very improbable, unless sociologically defined — that is, it is known that certain neurotic people commit antisocial acts in an attempt to resolve neurotic conflicts or problems; some of these people might have **27** and **72** codes, but the motivations behind their behavior are quite different from those of the true psychopath.

Suicidal thoughts and tendencies are often a possibility for persons with this code. In cases of severe depression, this code type has a good prognosis for electroshock therapy except when scale **2** or **8** exceeds 84 or more than four clinical scales exceed 80 (see Article 60 in Welsh and Dahlstrom, 1956).

Among Guthrie's medical patients there was little stress on physical complaints by the **27**'s. Half of them were seriously depressed, and the rest had strong symptoms of depression warranting such diagnostic terms as effort syndrome, fatigue, and exhaustion. Psychasthenic trends of rigidity and excessive worry were frequent among the men. The item analysis showed them to be unhappy with themselves and uncomfortable with others. They complained of brooding and loss of self-confidence and of a marked loss of efficiency and initiative. Contrary to expectation the subjects in this group did not respond well to treatment, nor was there evidence of spontaneous recoveries as is so frequent with mild depressive disorders. For the most part their condition remained fixed over protracted periods of time.

Among college counselees the total profile of the **27** group tends to be elevated; they present various problems related to home conflict, and the **72**'s were characterized as tense and indecisive.

Halbower's group was described as intelligent, having feelings of inferiority, inadequacy, and insecurity, with a strong need for personal achievement and recognition. They also showed self-blame, withdrawal, and obsessiveness-compulsiveness. They differed from the psychiatric group described previously in not showing psychotic or bizarre symptoms.

Marks and Seeman and Gilberstadt and Duker have discussed the **27**'s, the **274**'s, and the **278**'s, although their criteria for profile inclusion differed somewhat. The results of their research for the **27**'s were surprisingly similar even though Marks and Seeman included both males and females and inpatients and outpatients and the Gilberstadt and Duker group consisted only of male inpatients. Both groups were described as depressed, anxious, tense, nervous, weak, tired, and fatigued. Both groups had eating problems such as anorexia or weight loss and both groups had sleep disturbances. They had somatic manifestations of anxiety such as diarrhea, chest pain, nervous stomach, dizziness. They seemed to be perfectionistic, compulsive, striving to do well. They may have been ruminative or phobic, or have had obsessive thoughts. Gilberstadt and Duker preferred the diagnosis of anxiety reaction whereas the primary Marks and Seeman diagnosis was depressive reaction, but the secondary diagnoses seem to be the same. Gilberstadt and Duker's **274**'s differed from Marks and Seeman's group primarily in the high percentage of alcoholics (96 percent as compared to 10 percent). Otherwise the two groups differed from the **27**'s primarily in showing various passive-aggressive traits such as hostility, dependency, suspiciousness, impulsivity, insecurity, and need for attention. The Marks and Seeman group seemed to show relatively good response to psychotherapy compared to the Gilberstadt and Duker group where psychotherapy was largely ineffective.

Marks and Seeman described the **278**'s as chronically manifesting multiple neurotic symptoms which often masked thought disorders. They often overreacted to minor matters, were generally fearful, and were characterized as worriers. Often there was the neurasthenic syndrome, i.e., fatigue and loss of interest and initiative. Depression, manifested by feelings of hopelessness, and guilt-ridden self-accusation frequently were also observed. They tended to be obsessive, self-analytical, and ruminatively introspective. A principal mode of defense was intellectualization. They frequently suffered from indecision, often fearing to commit themselves to any course of action.

The basic personality pattern of the **278** was said to be schizoid, since these people were shy, withdrawn, and inhibited with poor heterosexual adjustment. Fifty-eight percent were diagnosed as schizophrenic, 33 percent as anxiety and obsessive-compulsive neurotics, 4 percent schizoid, 4 percent brain disorders. The **278** patients often responded well to tranquilizers and 50 percent showed decided improvement in treatment. The best treatment appeared to be a brief and goal-directed one which deemphasized introspection and encouraged the solution of real-life problems.

Gilberstadt and Duker reported the same constellation of complaints and symptoms and their **278**'s were diagnosed either as pseudoneurotic or chronic undifferentiated schizophrenia or as anxiety reaction or depressive reaction in schizoid personality. They were often mis-diagnosed as neurotics and if treated as such showed little improvement. They were described as ambivalent, unable to love, frequently unmarried. They have pan-anxiety, and are shy, quiet, withdrawn, obsessive, ruminative, and sensitive. Their thinking may be bizarre and their affect flat. They may suffer from severe depression, fatigue, weakness, insomnia, and apathy. They are sometimes perpetual students, and may have strong feelings of inadequacy and inferiority, be indecisive, and show somatic symptoms of anxiety. They often show interest in reading and ruminating about obscure subjects or religion and may have brief acute psychotic episodes and demonstrate ideas of reference.

28 and 82 Codes

The **28** and **82** codes were notable only in the psychiatric patients, where depression, anxiety, or agitation was found in the majority, and in a strong minority, hysterical tendencies (usually, however, excluding pain) such as conversion, paralysis, and blindness. The pre-illness personality of these subjects was described as unsociable. There was "mental loss" in the sense that the patient complained he could not concentrate, or there was psychometric evidence of deficiency or he said he was confused, or others said he was becoming inefficient in carrying on his activities. These patients were hypochondriacal and suspicious or sensitive. Heredity, defined simply as psychosis in siblings or parents, tended to be unfavorable in these persons.

A majority of these patients were psychotic diagnostically, actually more often psychotic depressions than schizophrenias. Almost all the neurotics in this group were diagnosed as mixed psychoneurosis, or, less frequently, as reactive depression. Hysteria did not occur and hypochondriasis was extremely uncommon. These patients were not psychopaths.

Schizoid features were noted in the medical patients with **28** codes, but seldom was a clear schizophrenic break reported. Confusion and apathetic indifference were the most frequent manifestations. The severity of the personality difficulties corresponded well with the elevations of profiles in this group.

Marks and Seeman's **28**'s and **82**'s were described as severely depressed with some retardation of the stream of thought and suicidal threats or ruminations. Self-esteem was low and these individuals often appeared tense and apprehensive. When anxiety, irritation, and agitation were present, it usually represented the turmoil of a person grappling with highly conflictual problems for which he saw no satisfactory solution. Common conflicts concerned emotional dependency, self-assertion, and sexuality. When anxiety and agitation were absent, as was typically the case, these individuals were described as resigned to their psychosis.

Thought processes were disturbed with obsessive-ruminative thinking occurring frequently. Hallucinations, both auditory and visual, may have been present as well as delusions of persecution. The resulting status was often of confusion, marked inefficiency, and inability to concentrate. The subjects' approach to problems tended to be stereotyped and unoriginal. Cognitive and intellectual activities were not highly valued, with aspiration and need to achieve being low.

These individuals tended toward withdrawal dissociation. They were introverted, and their approach to life was one of indifference and apathy. Social contacts were avoided since these people tend to be socially insecure and deeply afraid of interpersonal relationships. They were distrustful of people in general and tended not to become involved with others or in social activities.

Individuals with this code type were defensive about admitting that psychological problems existed; therefore, psychic conflicts were represented by somatic symptoms. Somatic delusions, difficulty in going to sleep, and weakness and easy fatiguability were often experienced. The physical symptoms were commonly more bizarre than those seen in the conversion symptoms. There was appreciable secondary gain from the somatic symptoms. Marks and Seeman found that 70 percent of their sample were classified as schizophrenic, schizoaffective type, but other writers have found the majority of their cases to be psychotic depressions. One study claimed that 28's are predominantly depressed whereas the 82's are predominantly schizophrenic.

Gilberstadt and Duker have described a group of patients with the 824 code which seems to be somewhat similar to the 842 and 482-824 group described by Marks and Seeman (see the section on 48-84). The cardinal features of this group were extreme irritability, hostility, and tension. If married the subjects showed severe marital maladjustment, and sexual psychopathology was a major problem. The sexual difficulty in marriages occurred in a context of extreme dependency and accompanying hostility toward spouses. Many of these patients were concerned about the acting out of other persons despite the fact that they frequently acted out in similar ways with alcoholism and fighting. Although psychopathic acting out was apparent on the surface, pervasive and apparently deep-seated guilt in conjunction with tendencies to deteriorate into frank psychosis over time indicated the malignancy of the underlying psychopathology.

In the backgrounds of these patients was a history of overly close, frequently seductive interactions with the mother due to the absence of the father in the home as a result of death, divorce, illegitimacy, or desertion and, frequently, the absence of siblings. There was often a history of poor school adjustment, with interpersonal difficulties and grade failures despite adequate intelligence. In some cases there was a history of childhood sickness and resulting overindulgence by the mother. Vocational maladjustment was frequent. These patients were lacking in drive, irresponsible, and occupationally very insecure. Aspiration for college and specialized training was frequently indicated, but there was not sufficient ego strength to complete these goals successfully. The modal occupation was bookkeeping or accounting. Strong feelings of failure were attached to vocational maladjustment.

29 and 92 Codes

Although there seems to be psychological contradiction in this high-point pairing, the **29-92** pattern appears with sufficient frequency in both normals and psychiatric populations to suggest that neither scale **2** nor scale **9** is unidimensional. Often the manic features are most prominent, serving to hide the depressive upset from outside observers and even from the subject himself; internal tension is a notable feature of their symptoms. The combination usually appears at a time when the manic mechanisms are no longer effective either in keeping the environmental pressures from overwhelming the patient or in distracting him from his mounting depression and tension. The pattern reflects serious illness especially when scale **9** exceeds the primed level.

Guthrie noted that the medical patients showing this code type were not described as depressed. Rather they showed a picture of tension and anxiety, the tenseness at times related to upper gastrointestinal complaints or to fatigue. Alcoholic histories appeared for men with this pattern. None of these patients was in serious difficulties and none visited a physican frequently. They responded quite well to the physical therapies used by the internist.

Hathaway and Meehl also noted the occurrence of this pattern in patients with organic deterioration of the brain.

Drake found aggressive or antagonistic behavior in college counselees with the **29** pattern. However, the most significant description for the females with this code was socially insecure. They were also seen as lacking self-confidence, tense, tense on examinations, unhappy, worrying a great deal, having insomnia, and rationalizing a great deal.

34 and 43 Codes

These codes are not very common and seem to occur in the "normal" population about as often as in psychiatric groups. Some research studies have dealt with these codes separately but it is not known whether the differences found between the two code groups are a function of the relative elevations of the **3** and **4** scales or whether these differences are a function of the clinical population being studied. In general the **34** code seems more frequent in women and the **43** code more common among men.

Among Guthrie's medical patients the **34**'s were mainly women and were similar to the **36**'s. They had numerous presenting physical complaints, none of which were acute or incapacitating. In interviews they concentrated on their symptoms and minimized emotional factors. The item analysis suggested a superficial outlook on life and inability to recognize the shortcomings of either themselves or their friends; they expected themselves and others to be perfect. None of these patients showed either frank asocial psychopathic or paranoid features. However, their interpersonal relations were tenuous and many expressed a well-rationalized hostility toward members of their immediate family. The **43**'s in this medical group showed some psychopathic tendencies, including alcoholism, marital disharmony, and sexual promiscuity. Their physical complaints were mild, episodic, and with little basis in physical pathology. Many showed an alteration in their histories between periods of acting out and hysterically determined illness.

Black studied a small group of college women with **34** and **43** codes. They were described only as impatient and were rarely called conventional, dependent, peaceable, or relaxed. They described themselves as energetic, frivolous, incoherent, talkative, and reasonable.

Welsh and Sullivan reported on a group of **34**'s who tended to be called passive-aggressive, passive type. They felt the magnitude of scale **4** reflected the aggressive or hostile feelings and impulses, while the scale **3** elevation showed that repressive and suppressive controls were even stronger. Consequently, the aggressions these persons would otherwise be expected to show intensely were kept from direct expression, appearing only obliquely, ineffectually, or sporadically. When aggressive actions toward others did appear, these persons often denied hostile intent, showing lack of insight into either the origins or the manifestations of their behavior.

Gilberstadt and Duker reported on a group of **43**'s in their **VA** population. The most outstanding trait of this group was poorly controlled anger which resulted in temper tantrums, most frequently associated with sensitivity to rejection but also frequently associated with inability to tolerate the frustration of immature, egocentric demands for attention and approval. When turned outward, the expression of anger frequently took the form of aggressive outbursts in which patients attempted to choke wives or children and made homicidal threats. When turned inward, anger took the form of impulsive suicidal threats. Somatic symptoms such as headaches, blackouts, or eye difficulties were frequent. Their fathers were described as rejecting, alcoholic, or absent. This group frequently had poor marital, job, and school adjustment, but some were successful in work as salesmen. Gilberstadt and Duker felt they would be diagnosed as emotionally unstable personality with conversion reactions or passive-aggressive personality, aggressive type.

Other studies such as Sines's and Persons and Marks's have shown that hostile, aggressive behavior is a regularly noted characteristic of men with the **43** code in state prison, state hospital, and university medical settings.

The **34** and **43** codes have been noted quite frequently among married couples, particularly where they are parents of disturbed children or they are being seen for marriage counseling. Individuals with this code seem to have the kinds of personality characteristics that tend to embroil them in marital difficulties. These difficulties may be characterized, in part, by a tendency to discharge anger and frustration onto a marital partner but without the communication skills (or inclinations) that would help resolve the conflict inevitably resulting. They have problems relating to impulse control, finding it difficult to give direct expression to their aggression in appropriate ways. Marital partners with such traits tend to avoid direct confrontation or direct expression of their anger and resentment in their interaction. They tend, rather, to discharge their negative feelings onto their partners indirectly by such subterfuges as innuendo, procrastination, or noncompliance tactics – all the while denying any negative intent. Their resentment may build up over time and emerge with an explosiveness and intensity far greater than merited by the specific occasion that triggered the outburst. The cumulative effect, in a relationship, of such "gunnysacking," the storing up of grievances, accompanied by periodic inappropriate outbursts, is the systematic decomposition of a relationship without either the communication skills or the honest admission of personal culpability to assist in its repair.

36 and 63 Codes

The medical patients with **36** codes were noted to be much like those with **34** codes, that is, mainly women with gastrointestinal symptoms. However, headaches, conspicuously absent in the **34** group, did occur among the **36** women. These patients each showed a single complaint, rather than an array of symptoms, but like the **34** group their conditions tended to be not serious, acute, or incapacitating. About half of the cases had histories of abdominal surgery.

Most of these patients were moderately tense and anxious. There was no evidence of paranoid delusions or even prepsychotic conditions. Rather, the paranoid element appeared as deep and often unrecognized feelings of hostility toward members of the subject's immediate family. Where there was awareness of these hostilities toward a parent or marriage partner, the feelings were clearly rationalized. Although their symptoms were well established and fixed, these patients continued to seek medical help.

The medical patients with **63** codes were described as rigid, worrying, defensive, and uncooperative. They resented any implication that their difficulties were psychogenically determined, and usually failed to return to the internist's office when this was suggested. They had histories of medical shopping from one physician to another. Paranoid features were frequently apparent on the first contact; several subjects were considered to be clearly prepsychotic.

Although these codes are relatively uncommon, Forsyth and Smith reported on a group of **36** nursing students. These girls were seen as being emotional, well thought of, continually asking questions, over-sympathetic, not allowing anger to be expressed, and uncomplicated. They were also seen as rarely manipulative and having few problems with authority.

Arnold found that the **36-63** codes were more frequent among his sample of "normal" couples than among those seen for marriage counseling. He suggested that in normal couples some of the conflict and stress of life — including the marital relationship — is apt to be either channeled into mild somatic symptomatology or overlooked as a function of the mild levels of repressiveness and denial reflected in scale **3**. Apparently even when frustration and hostility are present they are expressed in impunitive ways. Persons with this pattern are not apt to be direct and confrontive in the relationship, but neither are they apt to be openly or indirectly destructive of it.

38 and 83 Codes

Marks and Seeman have reported on a group of **38-83** females. These patients showed an acute onset of illness with depression or apathy, using unconventional thought processes and regression as a defense mechanism. Poor concentration, delusional thinking, affect distortion, rumination and overideational processes, hopelessness, resentfulness, and withdrawal were often characteristic. They were typified by poor prognosis and little response to treatment. About 48 percent were diagnosed as schizophrenic or manic-depressive psychosis; 45 percent were seen as dissociative or mixed psychoneurotic; and 10 percent were seen as schizoid. There were dissociative reactions in 40 percent of the cases. Some of them reported physical symptoms such as headache, blurred vision, numbness, chest pain, dizziness, parathesias, or eye complaints.

The **38-83** profiles are sometimes seen on a transitory basis with the person showing either clearly hysteroid or clearly psychotic symptoms at some other time. When grossly elevated this is one variant of the so-called "gull-wing" pattern seen in pseudoneurotic or chronic schizophrenia.

39 and 93 Codes

Medical patients with a **39** pattern presented histories of episodic attacks of acute distress. The attacks were marked by anxiety, palpitation, and tachycardia. The presenting complaints of **39** patients seemed to center about the lower gastrointestinal tract, the back, and the extremities. When they had intestinal cramps or headaches, the pains came on suddenly and intensely. On the other hand, ulcers, hypertension, and respiratory difficulties were virtually absent. Occasionally the medical problems showed a classic hysterical pattern, being both dramatic and medically atypical or impossible. The **39** patterns were frequently described as aggressive and as directing considerable hostility toward a domineering mother. While none of these patients had periods of severe depression in their histories, most of them were depressed and fatigued at the time they were seen. The physical problems of this group were not of a severe nature and readily yielded to superficial treatment.

Black's **93** college women were described in generally unflattering terms by their acquaintances. While the judges said these girls were sophisticated, they also labeled them dishonest, boastful, arrogant, show-offs, self-centered, suspicious, and flattering. In the long list of adjectives checked by these girls in their self-ratings, it is not possible to find any more self-critical terms than flattering and aggressive. They did not seem to sense the reaction they evoked in others, for they described themselves as popular, sociable, loyal, generous, and grateful. Although they said they were polished and poised (matching perhaps the sophisticated rating their peers gave) they also said they were affectionate, good-tempered, and reasonable, with wide interests. They described themselves as enterprising and energetic, courageous, and adventurous, cheerful and laughterful, alert and lively, and self-confident. In contrast to the terms indicative of high energy level and easy involvement in various activities, these girls also described themselves as peaceable, orderly, contented, adaptable, and practical.

Arnold found that the **39** and **93** occurred in about 10 percent of his "normal" husbands, but rarely in the marriage counseling group. He suggested that these men might be highly energetic and restless individuals who like to live life at a fast pace but who are apt, on occasion, to require medical intervention for acute but episodic physical ailments — perhaps induced, in part, by their highly active lives. They tend to channel an adequate portion of their energy, constructively, into their work and are apt to be highly productive — rather than exhibiting a pattern of starting many projects but finishing few as noted in the high **9**'s. Potentially, persons with this pattern would seem to be capable of marital relationships that are constructive, responsible, and marked by a lively diversification of interests and activities, although the "insensitivity-by-locomotion" phenomenon may produce misunderstanding and conflict at times with the marital partner.

46 and 64 Codes

Hathaway and Meehl's patients with this code tended to show depression, irritability, nervousness, introversion, suspiciousness, judgment defect, and alcoholism. About half of these patients were "conduct disorder" cases, behavior problems, criminals, and psychopaths of various kinds. Approximately a third were psychotic; the diagnoses were chiefly schizophrenia (most commonly paranoid) and a few paranoid states or paranoid involutional psychoses. Straight manic-depressive psychosis and schizophrenia of the hebephrenic form were rare with this code. Psychoneurotics were not common in this code group and tended to have reality-based, situational, or psychopathic elements in their problems; obsessional and somatization features, deep inner conflicts, and anxieties were lacking.

Guthrie's medical patients with **46** codes had varied physical complaints; this was true both for the patients as a group and for any given patient from one visit to another. Their physical and emotional difficulties were only vaguely described but some cases showed marked anxiety. When the profile was grossly elevated with a **46** pattern, the cases appeared clearly prepsychotic. There was a high incidence of asthma, hay fever, and hypertension, such symptoms in these cases being apparently related to instances of repressed hostility. The social maladjustment of these patients is noteworthy. In almost every case there was a report of seriously disrupted relations with the opposite sex, half of the women being divorced or in the process of getting a divorce. When the score on scale **4** was in the primed range, there was also evidence of poor work habits.

Marks and Seeman studied a small group of female **46**'s, 55 percent of whom were diagnosed paranoid schizophrenic and 45 percent personality disorder. Their most outstanding symptoms were hostility, tension, anxiety, irritability, depression, paranoia, and ideas of reference. They were also seen as evasive, defensive about admitting psychological conflicts, resentful, and argumentative, and using projection as a defense mechanism. Many of them had marital and sexual problems, and some had problems with alcohol or drug usage.

The **46** and **64** profiles are frequently found among persons seen for marriage counseling. Among the wives the pattern is often accompanied by a low score (< 45) on **5** and a high score on **5** among the husbands. In marital relationships a high degree of interpersonal sensitivity characterized by misinterpretation if not outright distortion of the mate's actions, words, and intention; projection of blame; selfishness and self-centeredness; anger and resentment; and an unwillingness to examine one's own deficiencies — all are frequently found with this code. In addition massive dependency needs seem to be reflected in this pattern, accompanied by angry, self-defeating demands and denunciations directed toward the partner. Complaining, whining, criticism — even when a valiant effort is made to please them — and an insatiable need for affection and emotional support are also concomitants of this pattern. There is a "double-bind" effect characterized by giving out of two contradictory messages or demands, neither of which can be fulfilled without disobeying or ignoring the second one. Such an individual is displeased no matter what the spouse does; the spouse is "damned if he does, and damned if he doesn't." "Normal" range elevations of this pattern suggest that the person is individualistic, verbally confrontative, and assertive — characteristics which at times might deteriorate into oversensitivity, blame, and insistent demand, but can potentiate open communication and perhaps other benefits for the marital relationship as well.

This code is also frequently found among adolescents, particularly female, and although one would not expect to find severe pathology among them, there is a somewhat greater probability of delinquency and dropping out of school than among average adolescents.

Marks and Seeman have also described separately a group of females with the **462** and **642** codes. These women were seen as anxious, depressed, tense, hostile, dependent, irritable, and immature. They were most frequently diagnosed as passive-aggressive and they were described as utilizing acting out as a defense mechanism, undercontrolling their own impulses, and acting with insufficient thinking and deliberation. Eighty-two percent were reported to have marital maladjustment, 42 percent extramarital relations, and 32 percent sexual delinquency. Suicidal ruminations and attempts, insomnia, sleep disturbances, somatic complaints, and loss of interest were also noted.

47 and 74 Codes

This code group shows an interesting internal contradiction in self-description; **47**'s indicate both excessive insensitivity in scale **4** and excessive concern about the effects of their actions in scale **7**. This psychological contradiction frequently appears behaviorally as an alternation of phases or cyclical variations. For a period these persons may act with little control or forethought, violating social and legal restrictions and trampling on the feelings and wishes of others heedlessly. Following such a period of acting out, however, they may show guilt, remorse, and deep regret over their actions and for a while seem overly controlled and contrite. Excessive alcoholic indulgence may be a part of these activity swings, as well as other amoral activities. While their conscience pangs may be severe, even out of proportion to the actual behavior deviations, the controls of these subjects do not appear to be effective in preventing further outbreaks.

Guthrie described a small group of women with this code who were tense and suffering from fatigue and a number of vague symptoms like headache, loss of pep, or pains in the stomach. They appeared to be dependent and insecure, requiring a great deal of reassurance. They had histories of family rejection or overindulgence. Although the number of visits made to a physician was above average, they obtained very little benefit from the simple reassurance or physical treatment given.

Marks and Seeman discussed the **47**'s with the **274**'s and **247**'s. (See the sections on the **24**'s and the **27**'s.)

48 and 84 Codes

Persons with this profile pattern are frequently described by acquaintances as odd, peculiar, or queer. They are unpredictable, impulsive, and nonconforming and the term schizoid personality is frequently applied to them. Their educational and occupational histories are characterized by underachievement, marginal adjustment, and uneven performance. Nomadism, social isolation, or underworld membership is often present. Crimes committed by persons with this profile are often senseless, poorly planned, and poorly executed, and may include some of the most savage and vicious forms of sexual and homicidal assault.

Among adolescents this code is quite frequent and probably does not have as severe implications as in the adult population (the normal range for adolescents may extend up to 80 T-score points) but there is a fairly high rate of delinquency with this code. The feature distinguishing between those with this code who do or do not become delinquent seems to be the stability of the home situation. The delinquent acts of the 48's and 84's differ from the aggressive antisocial behavior of the 49's; the former appear to be more the result of ineptness, misunderstandings, emotional conflicts, or simply following the gang. Some of these adolescents may be shy and withdrawn (check the 0 score) and possibly demonstrate peculiar mentation or behavior. Family problems, sexual confusion, and difficulty with authority are probably fairly common.

Marks and Seeman have described a group of patients with the 482-842-824 codes. These appear to be similar to the Gilberstadt and Duker group of 824 (see the discussion under the 28's). Among the Marks and Seeman group 71 percent were diagnosed paranoid schizophrenic and 21 percent sociopaths. They described a distress syndrome of moderate proportions, including symptoms of depression, nervousness, tension, insomnia, and anxiety. They appeared irritable, hostile, suspicious, chronically distrustful, and may have suffered from ideas of reference. They tended to be schizoid, in that they tried to keep people at a distance and to avoid close interpersonal relationships owing to their strong fear of emotional involvement. Projection, rationalization, and acting out were the usual defenses utilized by individuals of this type. Although they acted out in psychopathic ways with alcoholism, hostility, and perverse sexual behavior, some deteriorated into frank psychosis. Social intelligence was likely to be poor in this group, and serious difficulties could be expected in the area of empathy and communication ability. Persons with such profiles were often moody and emotionally inappropriate, and could not express emotions in a modulated adaptive way. In their behavior, they were characteristically unpredictable, changeable, and nonconforming, as well as argumentative, resentful, ruminative, and overideational. These individuals suffered from a basic insecurity and had an excessive craving for attention and affection. Immaturity, restlessness, feelings of inferiority, and feelings of guilt were also said to characterize these individuals. In addition, they tended to react to frustration intropunitively, to have feelings of hopelessness, and to have inner conflicts about emotional dependency. Psychological disorder was manifested in poor educational and vocational adjustment, and, if the subjects were married, in marital discord, including sexual difficulties and inner conflicts about them. Suicidal attempts and ruminations and alcoholism also occurred with this profile. The history of illness tended to be extended over at least a year and 30 percent of these patients were eventually committed. Regardless of type of treatment, one-third of these cases improved markedly, one-third slightly, and one-third showed no change. One would not expect large improvements as a result of psychotherapy, since these individuals were frequently described as lacking verbal-cognitive insight into their own personality structure and dynamics, as well as lacking "diagnostic" insight and awareness of the descriptive features of their own behavior. Their prognosis was generally considered to be fair to poor, although the presence of the high **2** did permit a better prognosis than in the **84** group. An elevated **0** was a good indicator of a schizoid process. When **0** was low, a characterological adjustment and an alcoholic father were strong possibilities. Maternal rejection and paternal indifference were characteristic of the **482-842** types.

49 and 94 Codes

Hathaway and Meehl's psychiatric patients with these codes were noted to be overactive, irritable, violent, talkative, extroverted, ambitious, and energetic. Three-fourths of these cases were psychotics, practically all manic except for some paranoid states, schizophrenia, and delirium tremens. A strong minority were psychopaths. Psychoneurosis, with the exception of a very rare severe anxiety state, does not occur with this code.

Guthrie's medical patients with **49** patterns were reported to be suffering from episodic periods of tension, sweating and dizziness, and anxious distress. They had histories of acting out behavior covering a wide range of troubles including marital problems, divorce, alcoholism, and illegitimate pregnancies. These considerations far outweighed their medical problems.

The medical patients with **94** codes did not present a homogeneous complaint picture, but rather showed general effects of tension and fatigue. These medical difficulties frequently followed clearly upon overactive and frankly hypomanic periods. The family adjustment of the 94's was poor and they had problems concerning their sexual adjustment. They did not stay in treatment long and therefore could be treated only superficially.

Both Gilberstadt and Duker and Marks and Seeman have described patients with this code type. About 80 percent of these cases were diagnosed as "personality disorder"; 15 percent of the cases were psychotic; while in no case was a diagnosis of neurosis or brain damage made.

These people were seen as avoiding close interpersonal relationships; undercontrolling their own impulses, resenting and resisting authority figures, self-centered, selfish, histrionic, self-indulgent, narcissistic, excitable, irritable, provocative, impulsive, resentful. They also showed low frustration tolerance, poor moral standards, poor work and marital adjustment, and were described as immature, irresponsible, poorly socialized, hostile, overactive, grandiose, moody, rebellious, extroverted, ambitious, energetic, violent, alcohol and drug prone, potentially delinquent. Acting out was the main defense mechanism used by these individuals, although rationalization also played an important role. These persons were well built physically and had corresponding athletic interests.

The childhood history of these patients frequently showed a dominant and overprotective mother who was unable to subject the child to any denials. This fact, coupled with a lack of identification with a passive father, may explain the low frustration tolerance, the need for immediate gratification, and the rejection of authority so commonly seen in adults with a 49 profile pattern.

These individuals tended to be young, to get married early. They showed a high frequency of unhappy marriages, illegitimate pregnancies, extramarital relations, abortions, sexual difficulties, alcoholism, drug use or addiction, delinquency and criminal records.

This code pattern was one of the most common found among Arnold's marriage counseling cases, particularly the males. These people may show insensitivity, lack of empathic awareness or regard for the mate's needs, shallowness of commitment, unwillingness to "give" as well as "take" in the relationship, irresponsibility, and a tendency toward excesses. The pattern is particularly destructive of the marriage relationship if the scores are over 70 and if the spouse shows a quite different sort of pattern. Among high school and college students one must interpret this code with care since the "normal" range for these groups is probably much greater (70-80 T score is common). Among adolescents this code type has been associated with high rates of delinquency, but the other scales on the profile seem to have some bearing on the actual likelihood of delinquency (less with scales **3, 5, 7**, and greater with scales **6** and **8**).

Various studies with this code among "normals" have indicated that these people may be assertive or aggressive, socially uninhibited, individualistic, and desirous of variety and diversity of experience. This pattern has been associated with good prospects for the WAC and successful life insurance salesman.

68 and 86 Codes

Hathaway and Meehl's psychiatric patients with this code showed primarily paranoid delusions and also depression, apathy, irritability, and withdrawal. The majority of these cases were psychotic, chiefly schizophrenia, with some paranoid states (about half were either schizophrenic or paranoid). The neurotics were more commonly "dysphoric," i.e., characterized by neurotic depression, anxiety, or adult maladjustment, than somatic. There were some conduct disorders although not of the pure asocial, amoral variety.

Guthrie's medical patients with **68** codes were described as pre-psychotic with schizoid personality patterns. They were, however, making a marginal adjustment without hospitalization; physical complaints and preoccupation with health may have served to stabilize their precarious adjustment. They presented a wide variety of complaints which shifted from visit to visit. They also had many food fads and depended upon patent treatments and medicines. Their relationships with others were unstable and characterized by resentment.

Marks and Seeman reported on a group of **86-68** females, where the mean scores on **8** and **6** were over 90 and **7** and **2** were at least 70.

Sixty-five percent of these were psychiatric inpatients; 70 percent were diagnosed psychotic, i.e., paranoid schizophrenic, and almost 20 percent paranoid. Depression, suspicion, agitation, tension, paranoid ideas, and inferiority feelings were all noted in this group. Disorders of thought and paranoid mentation were prominent features. Depression, tension, and nervousness were colored by a pervasive hostility and suspiciousness. A delusional system was likely to be present. General and pervading apathy and behavior characterized by regression, disorganization, and autistic and bizarre associations were present. Grandiose ideas, narcissism, and unpredictable and changeable behavior and attitudes were likely. These persons distrusted people in general and used projection as a defense mechanism.

Gilberstadt and Duker described a group of **68-86** male VA patients as assaultive, suspicious, withdrawn, introversive, having blunted inappropriate affect, auditory hallucination, and bizarre paranoid delusions. They showed primary thinking disturbances characterized by confusion, poor memory, poor concentration, and forgetfulness, as well as secondary or accessory symptoms of delusion and hallucinations. Withdrawal, shyness, flat affect, and chronically unsatisfactory interpersonal relationships were usually described. On admission to the hospital assaultiveness or threatened aggression was frequent especially following heavy drinking.

69 and 96 Codes

This code type seems to be relatively rare in most groups, but Marks and Seeman have presented data on a group of females, 85 percent of whom were diagnosed as paranoid schizophrenic. They were described as suspicious, emotionally inappropriate, hostile, withdrawn, and autistic with delusions, hallucinations, sleep disturbances, and difficulty in concentrating also noted. They were described as unable to express emotions in any modulated adaptive way, overreacting to danger or making emergency responses in the absence of danger, afraid of emotional involvement with others and having inner conflicts about sexuality. They manifested considerable social difficulty at home and at work. Forty-seven percent were the middle children in the family with the father described as permissive and the mother as affectionate but strict. Their behavior was agitated and their stream of thought was frequently irrelevant, retarded, or incoherent. They tended to show poor judgment and feelings of perplexity and unreality.

78 and 87 Codes

Hathaway and Meehl's psychiatric patients with this code were significantly younger than the other patients. They showed primarily depression and introversion with some also described as withdrawn, apathetic, nervous, irritable, and worrying. These cases were about evenly split between neurosis and psychosis, the former having a slight preponderance. A small minority were psychopaths. The neurotics were mainly depression, psychasthenics, or "mixed," with very few somatizing forms present. Except for mania, all kinds of psychoses were equal in frequency.

Halbower has described males with **87** profiles, who were seen as tending to complain of worry and nervousness, and as being introspective, ruminative, and overideational. Typically their personality difficulties were chronic, with long-standing feelings of inadequacy, inferiority, and insecurity. They were unable to take a dominant or ascendant role in interactions with others but rather manifested passive dependence. Socially they were lacking in poise and assurance and did not show evidence of rewarding socialization experiences. They were not outgoing, optimistic, or euphoric but dealt with problems on an internalized basis. Somatic symptoms did not provide them with relief from their anxieties; they appeared to lack defenses which would serve in any efficient way to provide them with comfort or freedom from distress. They did not show ideational poverty, however, and their rich fantasies were frequently concerned with sexual problems. Their emotional difficulties frequently interfered with their judgment and they often appeared to lack common sense in everyday matters. Although these patients did not feel particularly defensive about admitting to their emotional problems and disturbances, they did not have a good prognosis for psychotherapy; they did not readily form stable, mature, or warm interpersonal relationships with the therapist and did not integrate what they learned or profit from their experiences. Gilberstadt and Duker also described a group of **78** males whom they regarded as characteristically obsessive-compulsive. They showed the frequent psychasthenic traits of guilt, feelings of inferiority, fearfulness, feelings of inadequacy, lack of confidence, conscientiousness, and particularly attacks of anxiety, tension, and depression when faced with life stresses, especially in the major areas of vocational and marital adjustment. Physiological symptoms tended to be those related to anxiety such as headaches, palpitation, back pain, chest pain, and hypertension. These patients frequently drank excessively in a deliberate effort to relax. Shyness and difficulty in concentrating suggested a schizoid element. In early life they were frequently dominated by fathers or older brothers; in some cases the mothers were dominating or rejecting. Inherent anxiety, fearfulness, and shyness may have played a major part in eliciting dominating and rejecting attitudes from other family members. The domination and aggressiveness of fathers and brothers were usually resented and resulted in dependency-independency conflicts, but they retained a strong masculine identification despite feelings of inadequacy in relation to masculine roles.

Drake and Oetting described the male college students with this code as introverted, self-conscious, or socially insecure, lacking skills with the opposite sex, nonresponsive or nonverbal due to a lack of knowledge or information, vague goals, confused, indecisive, unhappy and in conflict with mothers and siblings. The females had complaints of nervousness, insomnia, headaches, exhaustion, depression, lack of self-confidence, conflict with mothers, fathers, and siblings, and lacking skills with the opposite sex.

89 and 98 Codes

Guthrie's medical patients with this code had histories of periodic hyperactivity, following which they sought medical help as their depressions came on. Their behavior showed some variation, but schizoid features were not prominent. The **F**-scale elevation varied with the severity of their condition.

Gilberstadt and Duker described a small group of males with this code, who at the time of hospitalization were described as unmanageable, tense, and panicky. In addition to being hyperactive, they were vague, evasive, disorganized, and disordered by delusions, hallucinations, and flight of ideas. Usually they were suspicious and overtalkative and preoccupied with religion. Some of them became indecisive and withdrawn to the point of catatonic immobility and posturizing. If they remained excited they became hostile, demanding, dazed, and disoriented and tended to pace. Their histories showed vocational indecision, and poor job role identification. They were usually single but if married poor sexual adjustment, ambivalence, and divorce were common.

Marks and Seeman described the **89-98** female group as suspicious, irritable, disoriented, perplexed, hostile, withdrawn, and autistic. The women showed emotional inappropriateness, delusions, hallucinations, sleep disturbances, and difficulty concentrating. They were described as spending a great deal of time in personal fantasy and daydreams, ruminative and ideational, utilizing regression as a defense mechanism, and unable to express their own emotions in any modulated adaptive way. They were also distrustful, keeping people at a distance, avoiding close interpersonal relationships, and afraid of emotional involvement with others.

Clinical experience suggests caution lest this pattern be overinterpreted in adolescence.

7

The MMPI in Practice

The incidence of contributory psychological factors in patients seen by physicians in general practice has been estimated by various writers to be from 50 to 80 percent. The figure may be somewhat higher or lower in the various specialties. In schools, counseling centers, and other helping agencies the same psychological factors are of great importance. For many of these people with psychological problems, the MMPI can be a valuable aid in identifying the problems and understanding them better.

After a person has taken the test his answers should be scored and the profile coded before any interpretation is attempted. This makes it easier to think of the test results as a configuration rather than in terms of answers to discrete questions or elevations on individual scales. The use of codes also lessens the likelihood that the psychiatric category names given to the scales will influence the interpretation; then, too, with codes the interpretation is likely to begin with the test rather than with the individual and to include comparison of "test-similar" persons with regard to various behavioral characteristics.

As pointed out in Chapter 1, it is important to have as much information about the test subject as possible. Factors such as age, sex, education, and occupation are all important to consider when evaluating a profile. The current status of the subject should also be kept in mind, and the reason for testing him — whether he is a psychiatric inpatient, a patient in the office with a medical problem, a student in academic difficulties, a spouse whose marriage is failing. Then as one begins analysis of the profile he can determine whether the subject is similar to the original normative group or whether he can be appropriately compared to other groups. For example, a 69-year-old grandmother and a 17-year-old boy with similar profiles may have some characteristics in common but it would be more fruitful to compare them with more similar persons. It is also possible that the person being studied may belong to a subgroup in which a particular kind of "deviant" profile is common, for example, college men whose profiles are marked by a high score on scale **5**.

Next, the relative validity of the profile and the test-taking attitude of the subject should be evaluated. This will provide some preliminary clues about the patient's personality as well as aiding in the interpretation of the profile. Various aspects of this problem have been discussed in detail in Chapter 3.

A consideration of the two-digit code should follow, using Chapter 6 above as a reference for the common codes. If three or more scales are all nearly equal, it would be wise to look at the material on all the two-digit combinations involved. The commonest three-digit codes ordinarily encountered include the **123** scales in any order; **2**, **7**, and **8**; **4**, **6**, and **8**; **4**, **6**, and **9**. Although the various two-digit codes will be helpful, it is also worthwhile to study carefully cases with comparable three-digit codes in the clinical *Atlas* (Hathaway and Meehl, 1951a). The *Atlas*, as a matter of fact, can be consulted at this stage for profiles similar to the profile of any case under consideration.

After the validity and overall configuration have been evaluated, then the individual scales may be considered. Although sometimes the elevations secondary to the two high points simply round out the picture, in other cases they may quite radically change certain predictions. In studies of delinquents, for example, the presence of certain scales tends to reduce the potential for delinquent behavior; these have been referred to as "suppressor" variables. Those that increase the likelihood of delinquent acts have been called "excitatory" variables. The addition of **6** to **49** and **48** codes increases the likelihood of serious trouble as well as the likelihood of psychosis. On the other hand a low **9** decreases the probability of suicide with **27** codes. These are only some of the possibilities that should be looked for.

In the cases where the secondary elevations do not radically change the picture gained from the two-digit code but merely furnish further information, the discussion in Chapter 4 will be useful. Ordinarily scale **1** is thought of as an index of somatic concern and anxiety, scale **2** as a relative mood indicator; scale **3** suggests hysteroid personality variables; scale **4** dissatisfactions, family troubles, or antisocial behavior; scale **5** indicates interest patterns, as well as estimating behavior along the passive-aggressive and dependent-independent dimension; scale **6** is an indicator of sensitivity and suspicion, as well as revealing anger and resentment; scale **7** is an indicator of anxiety and obsessive-compulsive traits, scale **8** of unusual thinking or behavior, scale **9** of general activity level, and scale **0** of social interest and activity.

At some point the absolute as well as the relative values of the scales should be noted; these may modify predictions.

Obviously the interpretation of an MMPI profile can occur on several levels. After a generalized analysis of the profile of the sort discussed above one may wish to consider it in terms of a particular patient or client. Ordinarily there is a wide variety of information about the test subject on the basis of which one can draw a number of conclusions or make predictions. At this stage, then, one can study the results for what they add to the previous picture of the subject and what implications they have for a future course of action.

For the sake of discussion, medical patients with psychological problems may be divided into two broad categories:

1. Those with primary psychological problems. Some of these patients are likely to require treatment in a hospital or in an institution, or commitment, and others are patients whose chief complaint is some type of psychological distress such as tension, depression, anxiety, fatigue, or inability to cope with life situations, sometimes accompanied by physical symptoms which may be direct physiological concomitants of the emotional state. Here the MMPI may confirm or clarify the diagnosis.

2. Those patients who have a secondary psychological problem. This group includes patients with a primary physical symptom or complaint for whom the physican feels that some psychological problem is likely

to be either a primary or a secondary etiological factor. Such complaints might be symptoms of the type mentioned above, as well as those which would be classified as conversion reactions or psychophysiological reactions. The group includes patients whose symptoms have an established medical basis but for whom psychological factors play an important role in determining the severity and duration of the illness as well as affecting recovery or rehabilitation. It also includes patients with certain neurological, metabolic, and toxic conditions which produce psychological or emotional reactions. Among these would be the organic psychoses as well as some of the less obvious conditions caused by endocrine imbalance, for example. With these patients the main problem is usually assessing the effects of various psychological factors. It is probably safe to say that these factors are always present along with the physical factors. One cannot rule out either psychological or physical factors by any single technique or method. At times, however, the MMPI profile may suggest some new possibilities, or the fact of a fairly normal or nonneurotic MMPI profile may encourage the physican to continue his physical or organic workup further.

The MMPI can also be helpful in dealing with patients who have established physical problems. By coming to an understanding of the patient as a whole person the physician should be better able to estimate how the patient will respond to alternative procedures. Often the MMPI interpretation will suggest new avenues of treatment or management of some patients. For example, the depressed patient may need treatment for his depression or at least additional support and encouragement beyond the medical management of his problem. The person with a high scale **3** component, on the other hand, may be quite optimistic and show good response to treatment but have relapses or develop additional symptoms with new and recurring environmental pressures or emotional problems. The high scale **1** person will often tend to confuse the diagnostic problem by presenting numerous symptoms, some of which are valid and others possibly misleading or contradictory. The patient with an elevation on scale **4** may be unreliable about following treatment recommendations and may need to be impressed with the nature of his condition, particularly if it is serious.

The possibility of potential psychosis or psychotic mentation may also impose certain limitations on the therapies or techniques used with certain patients.

It may have been noted that very little has been said specifically about treatment or therapy in this book. It is obviously beyond the scope here to discuss the various treatments for psychological problems. The *Handbook* discusses many of the studies relating the MMPI to various treatment methods. However, with the continual addition of many new drugs and treatment methods this material can have only limited value. It would be best to use the MMPI as a diagnostic tool and to turn to other sources of information for help in deciding what kind of treatment is best.

In nonmedical situations where the interpreted MMPI is available to professional workers, similar problems can be illuminated by the MMPI:

1. Clients with primary personality adjustment problems. This group might include, for example, people with severe depressions; people who are unpredictably and irresponsibly impulsive; or people who inexplicably behave in an untoward manner.

2. Clients with secondary personality problems that make a major contribution to their social and personal problems. In the school situation this could include students in academic difficulty and those with problems of truancy and other misbehavior. In other settings, one might consider secondary personality contributions to marital difficulties, parent-child conflicts, vocational adjustment problems, people who complain of loneliness and dissatisfaction with their life, social maladjustment to certain medical problems (pregnancy, drug use, venereal disease). Here also one might consider the life-style characteristics within the normal range that contribute indirectly to adjustment problems: One would not try to solve problems by urging the high **8**, high **0** person into a vigorous social life, or by suggesting a sedentary and thoughtful vocation for the normal person with a high scale **9**.

In some subgroups of subjects in medical and other settings modifications in the use of the MMPI may be called for. The special cases of adolescents, couples with marriage problems, the aged, people from different ethnic groups, and disabled persons are discussed in the next paragraphs.

Particular caution should be observed in using the material in this *Guide* with adolescents. "Blind" interpretation of an adolescent's MMPI profile should be avoided whenever possible, and an interview with such a subject is highly desirable. Persons using the MMPI frequently with adolescents should become familiar with the material available in the books by Hathaway and Monachesi (1953, 1961, 1963). Ninth graders have mean T scores on scales **4, 6, 7, 8,** and **9** about ten T-score points higher than adults, so that on these scales particularly one should be careful in interpretation of deviant scores. Environmental circumstances might have much greater effects on score elevations than the personality of the individual being tested. Some of the items on the scales mentioned just above seem to relate particularly to adolescent experiences, so that the meaning of a scale elevation might be quite different in an adolescent as compared to an adult. Some of the materials in this *Guide* specifically relate to adolescents and are so designated; they should be helpful to those wishing to use the MMPI in adolescent groups. In administering the MMPI to a young person one should particularly check to see if he is able to read well enough to understand the items and special care should be taken to ensure that he will respond to the test in a valid manner.

Special use of the MMPI can be made with couples who are experiencing difficulties in their relationship. Interactional interpretation of the pair of tests often reveals areas of unrecognized abrasion or of outright incompatibility. This is true even when both MMPIs are more or less within normal limits. When one of the tests reveals a degree of concern, unhappiness, and distress and the other is completely free from indications of depression or anxiety, insensitivity and lack of communication are probably present in the relationship of the couple. If one shows a high scale **0** and the other a low scale **0**, it is likely that some of the dissatisfaction in the relationship will revolve around going out together, entertaining friends, and other areas of socialization. If one member of the pair has a very high **Es** score and the other a very low **Es** score, it is likely that the relationship will be characterized by mutual exasperation and growing discomfort. Some people have applied the same techniques of interactional interpretation to the MMPIs of entire families which are being seen for counseling. Looking at all the MMPI profiles of parents and their children over the age of 14 will sometimes reveal important sources of family adjustment difficulties. In looking at the MMPIs of people over the age of 70 some variation in interpretation is necessary. In these subjects it is almost certain, for example, as noted earlier, that an elevation on scale **4** does not represent impulsive and psychopathic behavior; a high **4** in people over 70 more likely represents a deep and pervasive dissatisfaction. Some psychologists will tolerate much higher levels of defensiveness in the elderly than in the general population; that is, fairly high elevations on **K** and especially on **L** do not necessarily invalidate the profile. It is also quite possible that higher levels of scale **2** can be accepted as being more or less within normal limits.

In interpreting the MMPIs of people whose cultural or ethnic background is very different from the Minnesota norm group extreme caution must be used. Hypotheses about personality and adjustment that are drawn from the MMPI records of blacks, American Indians, Spanish Americans, the extremely wealthy, seminarians, artists, poets, and dancers, isolated mountain folk, and other similar groups must be held very tentatively. If the client is from a foreign country, whether he is taking the MMPI in English or in one of the translations, reference should be made to the *Handbook* and other sources for guidelines. There are some scales in some languages which are very unreliable and which should not be used. Scale **5**, for example, is so very culture-bound that it is rarely successful in any translation. Most of the scales are usable in translation even in the face of wide cultural differences. Scale **2**, for example, seems to measure psychological depression in Spain, Taiwan, and other countries nearly as well as in the United States.

The *Handbook*, bibliographies, and perhaps expert users should be consulted in connection with all special groups — for example, prison populations, people physically disabled, and patients with various chronic physical illnesses.

There are times when a normal MMPI represents a deviant response pattern. One would not expect to receive a normal MMPI from a

subject who has experienced a recent significant death. There are
situations in which anxiety is the expected response and its absence is
significant. Most patients recently hospitalized for medical reasons
show some reactive depression in scale **2** and some somatic concern as
reflected in scale **1**; the complete absence of depression and physical
complaints in the MMPI for such people suggests an indifference to the
condition that may have serious implications.

A word or two on the philosophy of test use and interpretation may
be of interest. In the use of personality tests as well as other mental
tests one will occasionally meet the objection that the test invades
personal privacy. This is an important and significant question which
does not, however, apply in the case of clinical use of a test. In the use
of tests in research careful attention must be paid to the subject's right
to maintenance of his privacy. When as patient or client he is seeking
help, successful treatment depends on the invasion of privacy. That is,
inaccessible parts of his personality and adjustment must be explored as
thoroughly as inaccessible parts of his body and its functioning. This
must, of course, be done in the context of professionally maintained
confidentiality, protection of individual rights, and ethical use of
private information.

When predictions are made about the future behavior of individuals
or about the subsequent course of their adjustment, the same
considerations apply. The user of the test must have knowledge of the
relative frequencies of what is being predicted. For example, many
suicides have **27** profiles, but the frequency of suicide is very low
compared with the frequency of **27** profiles. Further clinical information is needed to predict suicide or to act on its probability. It is
essential to remember that interpretive statements about the MMPI or
any other tests are always in the form of hypotheses and probability
statements.

A problem that often arises when using the MMPI is whether to
discuss the results with the test subject. Many people are curious or
anxious to know the results of the testing. It is important to recognize,
however, that direct interpretation of an MMPI profile to a patient can
be exceedingly difficult and risky. Psychiatric terminology is confusing

and carries many adverse connotations for most people. A test subject may misunderstand the direct interpretation or may feel that it incriminates him or shows him in a bad light. Accordingly, he may reject the test results and the diagnosis either implied or stated by the test results. This can certainly complicate the treatment to say the least. Any discussion of test results with a subject should be motivated by a good reason and not done just to satisfy idle curiosity or to impress him. In some cases it can be helpful if the person acquires the additional understanding of his problems that may be gained through discussion of the test results. In other cases such discussion might be helpful in explaining a particular recommendation or particular treatment plan.

If the results are discussed with the test subject, this should be done by the physician, by the primary therapist, or by a psychologist. The results should not be discussed by those who have only secondary or casual access to the interpreted MMPI. Planning and preparation should precede this discussion. The profile should not ordinarily be shown to him nor should specific scale names or scores be used in the discussion. The interpretation of the results should be expressed so he can understand it and should be as directly relevant to his particular problem as possible. In addition to the problems of confidentiality, which all professionals should be aware of, these cautions should also be kept in mind in talking with relatives or other interested persons about the MMPI.

The "sandwich" technique is often useful in presenting the information. The unfavorable or more "loaded" statements can often be sandwiched in between more favorable personality descriptions drawn from the profile. This also helps the person to regard the test giver and the test more favorably since it emphasizes that an effort is being made really to understand him rather than simply to pin a label on him. The physician or other professional can then proceed to relate these statements to the nature of the problem and go on to his conclusions or to the possibilities for treatment or further study.

Special care should be exercised in discussing with a test subject a computer printout interpretation of his test scores. Various automatic scoring and computer printout interpretations of MMPIs are available.* This means that the individual professional using the MMPI has a computerized "blind" psychologist as consultant. The various printout systems are widely different one from another. Some are more personalized, some are elaborate and complex, some are fairly simple probability statements. It is important to remember that the computer printout interpretations represent totally blind interpretations. They are comparable to those which a psychologist trained in the test would produce if he knew no more about the patient than sex and age. Anyone using these interpretations should augment them with extra test information and take them with a grain of salt. Characteristically these interpretations make two opposite errors. On the one hand they may express a great deal more pathology than is warranted; on the other hand they may express less. Still, used with caution, computer interpretations of the MMPI may offer suggestions and interpretations that the inexperienced user might otherwise overlook.

In general with the MMPI, as with all other diagnostic tests and techniques, experience is likely to be the most important factor in its application and interpretation. Through experience with his own clients or patients the user can best acquire the knowledge that will enable him to utilize the MMPI effectively, so that it makes a genuine contribution to his practice. Becoming well acquainted with computer printouts, with handbooks and guides, and with other aids to interpretation is a very good place to start in using the MMPI but a very bad place to stop.

----

*MMPI computer interpretation services currently available include the following (consult these sources for further information): Clinical Psychological Services, Inc., Los Angeles, California (based on a system developed by Alex Caldwell); Finney Institute for the Study of Human Behavior, Inc., Lexington, Kentucky; Institute of Clinical Analysis, Los Angeles, California (based on a system developed by E. Dunlop); Psychological Corporation MMPI Reporting Service, New York, N.Y. (based on the Mayo Clinic system); and Roche Psychiatric Service Institute, Nutley, New Jersey (based on a system developed by Raymond Fowler).

REFERENCES AND INDEX

References

The starred references below are the essential references for anyone who plans to use the MMPI extensively in practice. Each of these is followed by a brief description of its content, so that the user can determine which of these might be especially helpful for his needs. The *Handbook*, vols. I and II (Dahlstrom, Welsh, and Dahlstrom, 1972, 1974), contains recent, more complete bibliographies of the MMPI literature.

Alexander, F. The influence of psychological factors upon gastrointestinal disorders. *Psychoanalytic Quarterly*, 1934, 3, 501-588.

Arnold, Paul D. Marriage Counsellee MMPI Profile Characteristics with Objective Signs That Discriminate Them from Married Couples in General. Ph.D. dissertation, University of Minnesota, 1970.

Black, J. D. The Interpretation of MMPI Profiles of College Women. Ph.D. dissertation, University of Minnesota, 1953 (included in part in Welsh and Dahlstrom, 1956, Article 62).

*Butcher, J. N., ed. *MMPI: Research Developments and Clinical Applications*. New York: McGraw-Hill, 1969. A collection of recent articles, which is a useful adjunct to *Basic Readings*.

*Butcher, J. N., ed. *Objective Personality Assessment: Changing Perspectives*. New York and London: Academic Press, 1972. Another recent collection of articles.

*Dahlstrom, W. G., G. S. Welsh, and L. E. Dahlstrom. *An MMPI Handbook*, revised ed., vol. I: *Clinical Interpretation*; vol. II: *Research Applications*, Minneapolis: University of Minnesota Press, 1972, 1974. A basic, comprehensive, complete, and indispensable handbook for the professional user.

Drake, L. E. MMPI profiles and interview behavior. *Journal of Counseling Psychology*, 1954, 1, 92-95.

Drake, L. E. Interpretation of MMPI profiles in counseling male clients. *Journal of Counseling Psychology*, 1956, 3, 83-88.

*Drake, L. E., and E. R. Oetting. *An MMPI Codebook for Counselors*. Minneapolis: University of Minnesota Press, 1959. A codebook based on male and female college students applying for help to a large university counseling center.

Duker, Jan. The Utility of the MMPI Atlas in the Derivation of Personality Descriptions. Ph.D. dissertation, University of Minnesota, 1958.

Forsyth, R. P., and Sandra F. Smith. MMPI related behavior in a student nurse group. *Journal of Clinical Psychology*, 1967, 23, 224-229.

*Gilberstadt, H., and Jan Duker. *A Handbook for Clinical and Actuarial MMPI Interpretation*. Philadelphia: W. B. Saunders, 1965. A codebook based on male VA psychiatric inpatients in a large metropolitan VA hospital.

Gough, H. G., H. McClosky, and P. E. Meehl. A personality scale for social responsibility. *Journal of Abnormal and Social Psychology*, 1952, 47, 73-80.

Guthrie, G. M. A Study of the Personality Characteristics Associated with the Disorders Encountered by an Internist. Ph.D. dissertation, University of Minnesota, 1949.

Halbower, C. C. A Comparison of Actuarial versus Clinical Prediction to Classes Discriminated by MMPI. Ph.D. dissertation, University of Minnesota, 1955.

Hanvik, L. J. Some Psychological Dimensions of Low Back Pain. Ph.D. dissertation, University of Minnesota, 1949 (included in part in Welsh and Dahlstrom, 1956, Article 55).

Hathaway, S. R., and P. F. Briggs. Some normative data on new MMPI scales. *Journal of Clinical Psychology*, 1957, 13, 364-368 (reprints of this article are available from the Psychological Corporation).

*Hathaway, S. R., and J. C. McKinley. *The Minnesota Multiphasic Personality Inventory Manual (Revised)*. New York: Psychological Corporation, 1967. The basic manual.

*Hathaway, S. R., and P. E. Meehl. *An Atlas for the Clinical Use of the MMPI*. Minneapolis: University of Minnesota Press, 1951a. A reference collection of over 1100 case histories with associated MMPI profiles.

Hathaway, S. R., and P. E. Meehl. The Minnesota Multiphasic Personality Inventory. In *Military Clinical Psychology*. Department of the Army Technical Manual TM 8-242; Department of the Air Force Manual AFM 160-45. Washington, D.C.: Government Printing Office, 1951b. Pp. 71-111.

Hathaway, S. R., and Meehl, P. E. Adjective check list correlates of MMPI scores. Unpublished materials, 1952.

*Hathaway, S. R., and E. D. Monachesi, eds. *Analyzing and Predicting Juvenile Delinquency with the MMPI*. Minneapolis: University of Minnesota Press, 1953. A collection of pioneer studies.

*Hathaway, S. R., and E. D. Monachesi. *An Atlas of Juvenile MMPI Profiles*. Minneapolis: University of Minnesota Press, 1961. A representative collection of 1000 brief case histories of adolescents with accompanying MMPI data.

*Hathaway, S. R., and E. D. Monachesi. *Adolescent Personality and Behavior: MMPI Patterns of Normal, Delinquent, Dropout, and Other Outcomes*. Minneapolis: University of Minnesota Press, 1963. Report of a study of 15,000 young people with relation to various data including MMPI findings.

Hathaway, S. R., E. D. Monachesi, and Susan Salasin. A follow-up study of MMPI high 8, schizoid, children. In *Life History Research in Psychopathology*, ed. Merrill Roff and David F. Ricks. Minneapolis: University of Minnesota Press, 1970.

*Lanyon, R. I. *A Handbook of MMPI Group Profiles*. Minneapolis: University of Minnesota Press, 1968. A series of mean profiles based on MMPI scores of subjects in groups classified according to diagnostic or behavioral traits.

*Marks, P. A., and W. Seeman. *The Actuarial Description of Personality: An Atlas for Use with the MMPI*. Baltimore: Williams and Wilkins, 1963. A codebook based on male and female psychiatric patients in a large urban medical center.

Forthcoming is a new, expanded edition, P. Marks, W. Seeman, and D.L. Haller, *The Actuarial Use of the MMPI with Adolescents and Adults* (Baltimore: Williams and Wilkins, 1974).

Mello, N. K., and G. M. Guthrie. MMPI profiles and behavior in counselling. *Journal of Counseling Psychology*, 1958, 5, 125-129.

Navran, L. A rationally derived MMPI scale to measure dependence. *Journal of Consulting Psychology*, 1954, 18, 192.

Persons, R. W., and P. A. Marks. The violent 4-3 MMPI personality type. *Journal of Consulting and Clinical Psychology*, 1971, 36, 189-196.

Sines, J. O. Actuarial methods in personality assessment. In *Progress in Experimental Personality Research*, ed. B. Maher. New York: Academic Press, 1966.

*Swenson, W. M., J. S. Pearson, and David Osborne. *An MMPI Source Book: Basic Item, Scale, and Pattern Data on 50,000 Patients*. Minneapolis: University of Minnesota Press, 1973. A source book based on a population of patients at the Mayo Clinic, Rochester, Minnesota.

*Welsh, G. S., and W. G. Dahlstrom, eds. *Basic Readings on the MMPI in Psychology and Medicine*. Minneapolis: University of Minnesota Press, 1956. A reprinting of original articles on the theory, development, and use of the MMPI.

Welsh, G. S., and P. L. Sullivan. MMPI configurations in passive-aggressive personality problems. Unpublished materials, 1952.

Wiener, D. N., and L. R. Harmon. *Subtle and Obvious Keys for the MMPI: Their Development*. Advisement Bulletin No. 16, Regional Veterans Administration Office, Minneapolis, 1946.

Wirt, R. D., and P. F. Briggs. Personality and environmental factors in the development of delinquency. *Psychological Monographs*, 1959, 73, no. 15 (whole no. 485).

Index

Administration, 8, 9, 12
Adolescents, 25, 27, 29, 30, 33, 37,
    42, 75, 76-77, 80, 86, 89, 90
Age: minimum, for test subjects, 7
Alcoholism, 30, 54, 60, 64, 68, 69, 78
American Home Scale, 49
Anxiety, 25, 29, 35, 52, 53, 54, 64,
    66, 72, 78, 80
Atlas, 10, 23-24, 86

Booklet form, 7, 8
Box form, 7, 8
Brain damage, 68

Ca scale, 40, 46-47
California E-F scale, 49
California F scale, 49
Cannot Say (?) scale, 11, 12, 13-14
Carelessness: in taking test, 17
Caudality. *See* **Ca** scale
Clerical errors: in scoring, 17
Clinical scales, 5, 10, 11, 23. *See also*
    Scales **1-9**
Cn scale, 49
Coding, 6, 9, 10
College students, 25, 27, 28, 29, 33,
    35, 37, 39, 41, 72, 80
Compulsive behavior, 34. *See also*
    Scale **7**
Computer interpretations, 94
Configural analysis, 6
Conversion hysteria, or Conversion
    reaction, 28, 55, 56, 57, 72, 87
Conversion V, 45, 55

D scale. *See* Scale **2**
Delinquency, 8, 77, 86
Dependency. *See* **Dy** scale
Depression: and validity scales, 17;
    and scale **4**, 30; and two-digit codes,
    52, 53, 54, 58, 60, 62-64, 65, 66,
    67, 71, 72, 73, 80, 82, 87, 88, 89,
    92
Do scale, 47
Dominance, social. *See* **Do** scale
"Double-bind," 75
Drug abuse, 30, 60
Dy scale, 47
Dysphoric, 80

"Ego-strength." *See* **Es** scale
Electroconvulsive shock therapy,
    27, 63
Es scale, 44-45, 90
"Excitatory" variables, 86

F scale, 11, 12, 14, 17-19
F–K index, 21-22
Factor analysis, 41, 43
"Fake good," 15
Faking. *See* Validity scales
False-positive, 21
Form R, 7, 13
Frequencies, 24

Gull-wing pattern, 72

Handbook, 4, 11, 91
High-point codes, 10. *See also* Two-
    digit codes

23, 53, 58-60
231, 59
24, 60-61
247, 61, 64
26, 61-62
27, 31, 62-65, 92
274, 63-64
278, 63-65
28, 65-67
29, 67-68
31, 55-58
32, 58-60
34, 68-70
36, 34, 68, 70-71
38, 71-72
39, 72-73
41, 58
42, 60-61
43, 68-70
46, 32, 34, 73-75
462, 75
47, 35, 75-76
472, 61, 64
48, 76-78
482, 77
49, 60, 77, 78-80

62, 61-62
63, 70-71
64, 73-75
642, 75
68-86, 34, 80-81
69, 34, 81-82
72, 35, 62-65
74, 75-76
78-87, 35, 82-83
82, 65-67
824, 66-67, 77
83, 71-72
84, 76-78
842, 77
86, 80-81
89, 83-84
92, 67-68
93, 72-73
94, 78-80
96, 81-82
98, 83-84

Validity scales, 12

Welsh coding system, 11